Hidden Places
of Mann

by

Stan Basnett

Published by Leading Edge Press & Publishing Ltd,
The Old Chapel, Burtersett, Hawes, North Yorkshire, DL8 3PB.
☎ (0969) 667566
Fax (0969) 667788

ISBN 0-948135-39-5

A CIP Catalogue record for this book is available from the British
Library.

Edited by: Stan Abbott
Series Editor: Stan Abbott
Sketch maps by Stan Basnett*
Design and type by Tim Wright
Colour reprographics by Impression, Leeds
Printed and bound in Great Britain by Ebenezer Baylis and Son Ltd,
Worcester

* The sketch maps which accompany the walks are intended as a guide
only and it is recommended that the OS *Landranger,* sheet 95, is carried.
Better still, is the 1:25,000 scale Public Rights of Way map, published by the
Isle of Man Government, price £4.

Foreword

As I write this foreword, our Year of Railways, marking the centenary of the Manx Electric Railway, is getting into full swing and it seems an opportune time to repeat the message that the Isle of Man's railways are quite unique.

In the MER, the Snaefell Mountain Railway and the Isle of Man Steam Railway we can point proudly to working examples of Victorian and Edwardian engineering. The sheer scale of our operations makes Isle of Man Railways by far the largest vintage railway operator in the British Isles.

In all we have more than 37 miles of track, 22 miles of it double, and we carry about 170,000 people a year.

At a time when the Manx tourist industry must stand or fall on how well we promote the Island's rich heritage, our remarkable historic railways are an invaluable asset, as shown by the increasing share of the visitor market we are able to take on an unforgettable ride.

We are keen to support any initiative that will encourage even more people to discover the remarkable heritage of our railways and the stunning coastline and countryside they pass through.

In recent years, Stan Basnett's *Isle of Man by Tram, Train and Foot* has become something of minor classic and it is with particular delight that I welcome this sequel with the endorsement that permits it to bear our MER Centenary emblem.

I hope that, having come and ridden on our trains and seen our sights, you will encourage your friends to come and share the Manx experience.

Robert Smith
Chief Executive, Isle of Man Transport

References and illustrations

Place Names of the Isle of Man, II
Kneen
The Isle of Man — Memoirs of the Geological Survey of the United Kingdom, GW Lamplugh

Unless indicated, all illustrations are by the Author.

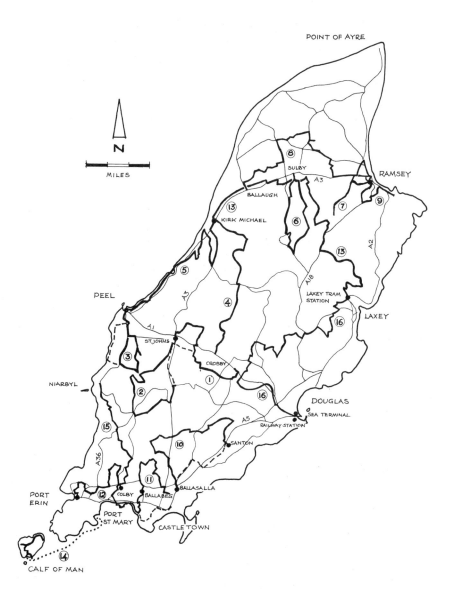

POINT OF AYRE

⑧
SULBY
BALLAUGH
RAMSEY
A3
⑬ ⑦ ⑨
KIRK MICHAEL
⑥
⑬ A2
⑤
PEEL
A3
④
A8
LAXEY TRAM
STATION
A1
⑯ LAXEY
ST JOHNS
③
CROSBY
① DOUGLAS
② SEA TERMINAL
NIARBYL
⑯
⑤ A5
RAILWAY STATION
⑩ SANTON
A36
⑪
⑫ COLBY
PORT ERIN
⑭ BALLABEG
BALLASALLA
PORT ST MARY
CASTLE TOWN
CALF OF MAN

N
MILES

*Map of the Isle of Man, showing the walks in this book (see also the
public transport map on page 41)*

Contents

This book is dedicated to Carol

...You know the turn
At the Bridge and the Chapel?
Well, in on the gate,
Behind there, that's the road, like straight
For Druid-a-whapple;
And just you're passin'
The School, and up you go—
A track—a track, you know,
On the side of the brew, criss-crassin',
Till you'll come out on the top like a landin',
And the house standin'
Two fields back—
And all that steep
You can't see the river, not the smallest peep,
Nor the gill, nor nothin'; but lookin' right over
At Snaefell,
By Jove! or
Barrule, or Slieu Core—
'Deed, you'll have to be cayful
With cows and the lek; and no road for a cart
Up yandher place,
But comin' in from another art,
About nor'-wes',
Ballaugh way? Yes.

From Kitty of the Sherragh Vane by TE Brown

Introduction

THIS second RailTrail book on walking in the Isle of Man is being published to coincide with the 1993 Centenary celebrations of the Manx Electric Railway.

The theme is similar to that of the companion volume, *The Isle of Man by Tram, Train and Foot*, combining, as it does, walking with the use of public transport. But, as the title suggests, it also takes us on our wanderings to some of the more unusual places on the Island. The book stands on its own, but it is intended as a companion to Tram, Train and Foot and for that reason, the section on the Island's pre-history is not repeated and the section on industrial and social history is expanded in other directions.

Walking certainly puts us in close physical contact with the land, while, at the same time, giving plenty of opportunity for thought. Why is that hill that shape? Why is there a valley here? and no river! What set the course of the rivers we see?

Many times have I posed these questions looking about the Island from favourite hilltop haunts. Perhaps I am a dreamer at heart, but a little investigation reveals a whole wealth of physiography all around us. With a little understanding of how the Island was formed, quite ordinary features suddenly take on a whole new meaning.

The rock formation of the Island is predominantly slate from the Cambrian period, formed from layers of mud and sand laid down beneath the sea and consolidated to form some of the world's oldest stratified rocks. Subsequent upheaval of the Earth folded the strata considerably and there are many places on the Island where this can be seen, the most dramatic examples occurring on the Marine Drive, south of Douglas.

The rock is interspersed with metaliferous lodes and the Island displays some signs of igneous (molten rock) intrusion, illustrated by numerous granite bosses, most of which are readily identified by the quarrying activity they attracted in the past and which is still evident at Poortown and Foxdale. The rock is crossed with numerous dykes, predominantly of greenstone. Scarlett, in the south of the Island, reveals the only visible remains of volcanic activity. Weathering and further movement broke down the slate in some areas, to resettle as conglomerate which can be seen in some coastal areas.

The physical features that we see today are directly attributable to the Ice Age, when the early formations were modified to leave the smooth rounded skyline of the hills, cirques, the glacial valleys, the dry rivers and the northern alluvial plain. It is all there — albeit on a small scale by world standards. The melting ice sheet left other traces in the north of the Island in the course of its reluctant retreat.

Many hollows contained inland freshwater lakes, and traces of these can still be seen, although man-made channels have drained most of the area to provide some of the best agricultural land in the Isle of Man.

Old maps showed a number of large lakes, some well over a mile long and at least half a mile wide. The largest was Lake Mirescog, to the north of the Sulby River, between Sulby and Ramsey. Its existence is well documented and records show that fishing rights were granted to the Bishop in the 16th century. Its name, Norse in origin, appears on later maps as Malar Lough and the name survives today as the Lough Mollo or Mallow Trench, a drainage ditch draining the area once occupied by the "Great Lake of the Plain".

The other two significant lakes were Lough Dhoo (the dark lake), corrupted through time to the Dollagh, and Loughan Ny Eiy (the pond of the geese). The existence of these lakes is only hinted at by the place names which still exist.

Remnants of the lakes remain in the Curraghs and the Lhen. Lough Cranstal, in Bride, is probably the best example left of what these lakes were like.

As for the rest? Well, they survive in place names as do the islands which existed within the lakes, on which stood small buildings and farmsteads. The Manx Gaelic word meaning island is "ellan", so present day farm names such as Ellan Bane (white island) and Yn Ellan Rhennie (the ferny island) clearly indicate their origin upon translation.

Altogether, reference to the map reveals 34 place names with Lough or Loughan in their description in the northern parishes and at least 12 names prefixed with the word Ellan.

Gradually, through natural silting and the efforts of individual landowners, some of the land adjoining the loughs was brought into cultivation. Tynwald, the Island's government, realising the potential of the northern plain, introduced the first meaningful Land Drainage legislation in 1763 for the enforcement of the proper drainage of "...loughs and stagnation of water in divers parts of this Isle..." Further legislation followed in 1776 and 1851 which made significant improvements in drainage. Eventually the Land Drainage Act of 1875 laid down the Drainage Districts and network of drainage ditches which still exist today.

The first attempt to introduce legislation dealing specifically with rivers came in 1851. This was consolidated in 1875, the next significant move coming with Land Drainage Act of 1934, following severe flooding throughout the Island in 1930.

The Laxey River caused major damage in the lower part of Laxey, aggravated by works associated with the Manx Electric Railway's power station. However, the Sulby River ran amok and I was told many stories of people taking to the upper stories of their houses, and indeed to the roofs of the cottages, near Sulby Bridge, where the flood water was some 12ft (3.6m) deep.

The Sulby River is the largest of the Island's main watercourses and takes its name from a Norse personal name. Before the floods of 1930 it was notorious for overflowing its banks in winter. In its formative years it discharged to the sea at the Lhen and then, over the intervening years, meandered its way over the northern flood plain eventually settling more or less on its present route.

During the Ice Age the Island was believed to be covered by an ice sheet more than 1,000 feet (300m) thick. As it retreated north in the late Ice Age, the ice sheet deposited much of the boulder drift which moulded the Bride hills and set the foundation of the northern plain. As the residual ice melted from the upland areas it added to the gravel in the flood plain, thus contributing to the formation of the lakes referred to earlier.

In 1916 "alien" labour from Knockaloe camp — described in Walk 3 — carried out extensive work on the banks of the Sulby and straightened areas in the vicinity of the railway bridge at the Garey. The Lough Mallow stream was also straightened and deepened. All of the work was done between July 26 1916 and December the following year, under the supervision of the Surveyor General, Mr W R Kay.

Extensive realignment and straightening of the river was carried out following the 1930 flood and the main rivers were vested in the Government for the purposes of maintenance. The river is now only a shadow of its former self, having been tamed by the building of the new reservoir at Tholt-e-Will.

The other main rivers are the Laxey River (the salmon river), the Neb, the Awin Glass (the bright river), the Awin Dhoo (the dark river) and the Awin Argid, or Silverburn (the silver river).

On our walks, we shall see many of the places described, and most of the features, including dry rivers and glacial valleys and that other phenomenon referred to in the Coastal Walk in Tram, Train and Foot, the raised beach.

Many of the roads and tracks on which we shall be walking were established by customary use and, up to the end of the 17th century, were no more than narrow green tracks repaired as necessary under the direction of the Captains of the parishes.

The first Highway Act was introduced in 1713 and for the first time parish overseers were appointed to ensure that main-tenance of the country roads was carried out by adjoining own-ers and taxes were levied to provide for additional labour and materials as required. Maintenance by "the public at large" meant precisely that, on penalty of a fine for non-performance.

In 1765, James Hamilton was appointed Supervisor-General of Highways. He was no stranger to the Isle of Man, having previously built roads for the Duke of Atholl. He was instructed by a Committee of Highways to build new roads to a width of 18 feet. Hamilton was responsible for laying down the network of roads existing to the present day, linking the principal towns and villages. He was a popular man and held in high regard.

By 1776, it was apparent that insufficient funds were avail-able to carry out the work required to improve the Island's roads. A new Highway Act was introduced in the same year, increasing taxes and laying down a standard width of eight yards for all highways. Overseers were abolished and replaced by Parochial Surveyors, responsible through a Surveyor General to a Committee of Highways.

Legislation has continued to the present day, with rapid progress dictated by the development of the motor car, although the standard width for a highway remains as laid down in 1776.

Prior to 1860, the status of roads over the mountain land was not clear. The Isle of Man Disafforesting Act of 1860 vested the Common Land in Commissioners, with power to create roads over the mountains and declare them public. Many were surfaced after 1923 but others remain to be explored by walkers and others, as a silent memorial to a former way of life linking mills, allotments, mines and providing access to the turbaries (peat-digging areas).

The right of access of the public to the mountains generally, was given statutory form by Section 32 of the Lords' Rents Purchase Act, 1913.

All of this gives an insight into the condition of roads and rivers within the Island in the middle of the 19th century, and to the difficulty of travelling about, which, for all but the very wealthy, was impossible and, even then, an ordeal. It is no wonder that the steam railway and the electric tramways flourished after their introduction in 1873 and 1893. Suddenly, the ability to travel was available to all. An hour to Ramsey instead of four and a half by stage coach, being bumped and jostled all the way. Can you imagine what it must have been like?

Now we become frustrated and angry if we are delayed for five minutes in our motor cars! Where are we all going in such a hurry?

Reflect on the changes that have taken place in the last century and a half. Imagine the arrival of the first steam driven vessel off the coast of the Island in 1815. By 1819, James Little and Company, of Greenock, was operating a coastal service to Liverpool, calling at Portpatrick and Douglas on the way. In 1822, the St George Steam Packet Company commenced a regular sailing between Liverpool and Douglas. Travel was transformed. Soon local businessmen wanted some of the action, so they formed the Isle of Man Steam Packet Company in 1830. It is still trading today, albeit in rather different guise and own-

SS Lady of Man, built in 1930 and certified to carry 2,873 passengers. Photographed leaving Queen's Pier, Ramsey.

ership, although the present vessel, the *MV King Orry*, at 4,648 gross tons and 370 feet in length, is a far cry from the first vessel, the *SS Mona's Isle,* of 200 tons and 116ft length.

The advent of the Steam Packet took the vagaries of the weather out of travel and regular sailings could almost always be maintained. As the Victorian era dawned, so we saw men of great vision take even greater chances with their money... and that of other people. Not every venture was successful, but the Island seemed to get its fair share. The Isle of Man became a sophisticated watering hole, a playground for the rich and the poor.

The Lancashire and Glasgow wakes were a feature of the holiday traffic which developed, and the opportunity of a boat trip across the sea, whose cost fell within the grasp of working class families, gave the Island the edge on other West Coast towns. The Isle of Man Steam Packet Co ordered its last purpose-built paddle steamer in 1897, from Fairfields, and named it *Empress Queen* to commemorate Queen Victoria's Jubilee. The vessel sailed between Liverpool and Douglas and regularly made the sailing in just three and a quarter hours. They were heady days and by 1899 the Island was enjoying the pleasure of 400,000 visitors a year. Yet still there was no motor bus service, a facility which had only just been introduced in London. The railway and the tramcar reigned supreme.

The Isle of Man Steam Packet Co celebrated its centenary in 1930 by building the *SS Lady of Mann*, which in many ways epitomised the development of the cross-channel steam packet vessel. This beautiful ship, after a distinguished career, was scrapped in 1971 and in true Island tradition outlived all her contemporaries.

Just when this ship was being built, air travel was in its infancy, and by 1933 Blackpool and West Coast Air Services were operating between an airfield at Squires Gate, Blackpool, and an airfield at Ronaldsway. A funny thing as I write this: I have just realised that you can still catch an electric tramcar at Fleetwood and travel to Squires Gate, fly to the Isle of Man and catch a train to Douglas. Perhaps not so much changes after all.

But it did. Ronaldsway was just a field, then the second world war came and it changed dramatically, being purchased at the end of hostilities by the Isle of Man Government to become the modern airport of today. During the war, there were aerodromes at Jurby and Andreas. Jurby continued to be operational as an Officer Cadet Training Unit until 1963. Andreas, on the other hand, closed in 1946 and reverted to farmland.

In 1935, the Hall Caine airport was built at Close Lake to compete with Ronaldsway, but it was only to last for two years. Think about the place name — an enclosure by the lake... but what lake? Sure enough, the airport was built on the flat land formerly occupied by the ancient Lough Mallow.

That nicely completes this verbal ramble, so perhaps we should get on with the real rambling. But, before we do, it is worth thinking about how we nearly lost our railway heritage.

I was right earlier when I wrote the words "the railways and tramways reigned supreme". In 1895 they respectively carried 830,263 and 1,843,697 passengers. Those annual figures were maintained more or less to the outbreak of the second world war as far as the steam railway was concerned, despite competition from bus operators. In 1937, passenger figures stood at 775,499. The tramways were not so fortunate, having suffered two major blows. The first was the collapse of Dumbells Bank, when directors of the tramways enjoying a similar role at the bank had overstretched the borrowing of one for the other. Apart from crippling the tramways, the consequences of the collapse had repercussions throughout the whole Island community.

The second event occurred in September 1930 when, as a result of exceptional rainfall, a patent automatic weir failed near the Laxey generating station, which resulted in claims exceeding £2m,

GLEN ROAD DAMAGED BY FLOOD. LAXEY SEPᵀ 18. 1930

The failed tipping sluices and some of the damage caused in Lower Laxey in September 1930. Claims against the Manx Electric Railway reached £2m.

from which the Manx Electric Railway Company never really recovered.

After surviving the second world war, the tramway enjoyed the post-war boom but suffered from lack of investment in the track and overhead supply, and competition from, once again, the bus operators. The most successful of these was Isle of Man Road Services, wholly owned by the Steam Railway.

Fortunately, the Isle of Man Government saw the value of the tramway as a tourist attraction and stepped in to buy the whole undertaking for £50,000 in 1957. The profitability of the Ramsey section was soon in question, and it had a very shaky few years. For a short time, the tramcars endured a change of livery to a rather clinical green and white but, by 1963, they had all reverted to the more familiar red and cream, with varnished panels on the closed saloons.

The steam railway had enjoyed continuing traffic levels throughout the war, including heavy mineral traffic to Ronaldsway for the construction of the new airport for the Royal Navy, and military traffic in connection with training and the movement of internees. This was all very well but, for six years, track maintenance was neglected and locomotives and stock were hard worked, with the minimum of maintenance, due to lack of manpower and availability of materials.

It was a tired railway that responded to the post-war holiday bonanza enjoyed by the Island, but respond it did and in 1945 the two networks carried 1,250,000 passengers, a level maintained for the next decade.

It was during the latter part of this period that my own interest in the Isle of Man Railway developed and why I think that the only colour for the locos is Indian red and that the coaches should be cream and red!

The next decade was to see many changes. Surely the one which has accounted for the greatest change in public transport was the motor car and its availability to everyone, together with the removal of petrol rationing.

It was clear that the railway was being seriously affected. Closure was mooted in three Transport Commission reports produced for the Isle of Man Government, the most recent in 1949. Somehow, the railway survived. In 1957, Sunday services ceased and winter services cuts followed in 1960/61, along with winter closure of the branch from St John's to Peel. Then, the following year, the service in winter was restored to Peel, but the line from St John's to Ramsey was closed. Locomotives No.10, *G H Wood*, and No.11, *Maitland*, carried most of the winter services with only one loco in steam at any one time.

By 1962, the railway was running less than 50,000 train-miles, a fifth of its immediate post-war mileage. Two second-hand diesel railcars were purchased from the County Donegal Railway in Northern Ireland, arriving at Douglas on the *MV Antrim Coast* during 1961. Suddenly, there was no steam operating in winter.

A 1961 view of Braddan halt on a Sunday where several special trains took visitors from Douglas to Kirk Braddan for the open-air church service. After discharging passengers, the trains proceeded to Union Mills where the locomotive ran around the train and awaited the end of the service.

Further reductions in service took place in 1964/5 with trains only operating to Port Erin in the winter. The end was in sight and 1965 proved to be the last full season operated by the Isle of Man Railway, with closure being announced in January 1966.

Fortunately, the railway struggled on with a leasing arrangement between the Company and the Marquis of Ailsa, who led a consortium of businessmen in a private venture which was to last only between 1967 and 1972 and then only latterly with Government aid.

After protracted negotiation, the Isle of Man Government did acquire the railway and most of its property but not before the Foxdale line, the Ramsey line and most of the Peel line had been removed and sold for scrap to a firm at Millom, Cumbria.

Ex-County Donegal Railway diesel railcars on the Peel line approaching Braddan Bridge in a snow storm, March 3, 1965.

The only section of the network which had remained intact and continued to operate was the South line. This is all that remains to the present day and it is now well preserved for the foreseeable future. So let's enjoy it while we can.

The following walks are all contrived with some link to the railways and tramways. You will need a bus/tram/train timetable, the latest edition of the Public Rights of Way map and a compass. Suitable walking gear and a rucksack are advisable.

The hidden pool

4 hours
8 miles

A quiet lake beside a forest gives a taste of the "hidden places" to come. Our walk ends at the historic site of the world's oldest parliament.

OUR first walk to a hidden corner starts at Glenvine. Take the No.6 bus from Douglas and get off at Glenvine where there are two places, worth a little time, depending on your interests.

There is the Manx Motor Museum, which is a private collection of historic vintage, veteran and classic motor vehicles, open to the public in the summer months and by arrangement at other times. A short distance away is the Garden of Mann Garden Centre, opposite the school. It is down the road past the school that our walk starts, soon crossing the disused track of the Douglas to Peel railway.

Dedicated RailTrailblazers may choose to add another four miles to the walk by taking the Heritage Trail from Douglas

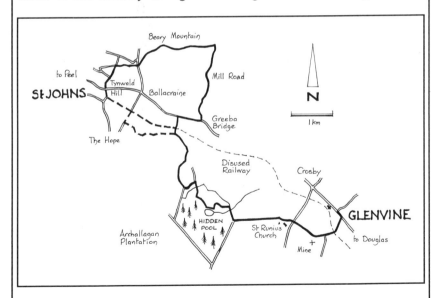

along the old railway line, to join the walk here. If you have not heard about the Heritage Trail, you can read a little about it on the notice board by the old gatehouse.

We continue along the road to its junction with Ellerslie Road, where we fork right and start to climb uphill, passing

Glen Darragh and the old mill and, a little further on, the remains of the Bishops Barony Mine which was apparently commenced about 1825 on the orders of the Bishop Murray. It had a
very poor production record during its working life and was in
ruins by 1900. Now all that remains is the chimney which can
be seen through the trees on the left.

Continuing up the hill, we pass Ellerslie farm, also on the
left. This was built as a model farm by Italian prisoners of war
during the first world war for the Cunningham family. The
remarkable centre building in the yard is a magnificent piece of
architecture in its own right.

Going straight on at the crossroads at the top of the hill, we
pass the old parish church of Marown and continue over the
rough made road to Eairy Kelly and the plantation. Along the road
we enjoy a view over the Central Valley, which is really only a
foretaste of what is to come.

Eairy Kelly is the building at the end of the road and we must
be careful to turn right into Archallagan Plantation. Once in the
car parking area, we are confronted with three gates: we go
through the one on the right and head off downhill into the plantation, soon emerging beside the boundary wall with a superb
view out to the right over Cooillingel, which was also part of the
Bishops Barony referred to earlier, and the valley down which
the River Dhoo starts to wend its way to Douglas. Almost straight
ahead of us is the broad front of Greeba Mountain and the King's
Forest.

The little stream we are about to cross is the River Dhoo (the
dark or black river), once across we continue along the forest
track beside the wall for a short distance before following the
track sharp left away from the wall and uphill through the
forest, which in winter presents a great variety of fungi.

Now we have to be careful as we emerge into a clearing. The
track divides and the main track swings right back into the
forest, but we take the left fork on the rougher track, skirting
the edge of the trees and swinging round in an arc to the left.
This part of the forest is by far the most beautiful, with its
mixture of deciduous and conifer trees providing an area open
enough for small birds.

Just as the track leaves the forest on the right and swings
further left and downhill, stop and climb up the bank on the
right to find our hidden corner!

The lake in the middle of Archallagan is man-made and built
on the source of the River Dhoo. Archallagan means "a little
height" according to Kneen's *Place Names of the Isle of Man* and,
although the meaning is obscure, there is no doubt that we are in
the middle of the plantation and the clearing is on the top of a

The strange silence of Archallagan. Slieau Whallian overlooks the pool which is our first hidden corner.

hill. It is an ideal spot to stop for a rest or a picnic... Strangely though, during all the times that I have been here I have never seen duck or geese or even a migrating swan resting here.

Having taken in the tranquillity of the area, we have to press on. We have to walk alongside the lake and quickly join the track alongside the forest, walking in the open with the summit of Slieau Whallian in the far distance. The track eventually dives into the trees and we find ourselves in the older part of the plantation, the track now being grass-covered and carpeted with pine needles. We shall follow it, crossing a newer track on the way but now going slightly downhill soon to emerge from the plantation at a gate overlooking Cornelly, or Townshend, Mine, last worked in 1886, and described in more detail in *The Isle of Man by Tram, Train and Foot*. There is a plaque which gives a brief description of the mine.

As we pass the mine, we turn right and follow the signposted right of way to Greeba, through Kerrowgarrow, passing beautiful views of Greeba (meaning "The Peak"), particularly by the ruined tholtan (farmstead) on the way down the left hand side of Glion Darragh (Oak Glen). The farmer at Kerrowgarrow has signposted a diversion into the field to avoid the usually very muddy section of the road leading into the farm. We walk through the farmyard, taking care not to take the road to the left, and soon crossing the old railway track before to join the main Douglas to Peel road, where we shall turn right to Greeba Bridge and left up the Mill Road.

But wait, if you are going to take this walk during June or September, the main road may well be closed for motorcycle or cycle racing. Don't despair — you can take that left at Kerrowgarrow that I told you about, through Kennaa Farm, with views over Beary Mountain, then dropping down to the Curragh Road, turning right to the railway track and left to St Johns, and the end of the walk at Tynwald Hill.

When the road is not closed for races, we can climb up the Mill Road, above Kerrow Glass (meaning "the green quarterland"), with splendid views of Greeba Mountain and Beary Mountain at the head of the valley. We continue to the gate at the top end of the surfaced highway.

We go through the gate and turn left along the Dowse Road, a rough track along the edge of Beary Park and the 12 shares, former shielings (pastures) now being brought back into culti-vation. The walk along the track commands views over the central valley and St Johns, with Slieu Whallian dominating the view ahead, particularly as we drop down through Ballig Plan-tation. From here, we carefully cross the main road and continue down the road opposite, through Tynwald Craft Centre, which is certainly worth a stop and a visit to the cafe.

The buildings here originally formed the large Tynwald Woollen Mills, built in 1920 to consolidate other mills in the area, operated by the Moore family and others. The enlarged mill was electrically operated and the boiler house can be seen at the end of the car park. Some limited weaving is still done on the premises and sold in the shop.

We continue to the crossroads by the bridge over the Neb and turn left to St Johns, arriving at the main road under the shadow of Tynwald Hill, site of the annual ceremonial session of the worlds oldest parliament. We are going to catch the bus back to Douglas from here, but while we wait, we can read the descrip-tive plaque below the hill and perhaps visit the church, if time permits.

Witches, windmills and waterfalls

4 ½ hours
9 ¼ miles

A good mixture of track and moorland, taking in a summit with an ancient hill fort and some of the best views in Mann.

STILL using the old Peel line as our tenuous link with the RailTrail theme, we start this walk at St Johns, having taken the No.6 bus from Douglas.

From the bus stop, we make our way down Station Road, opposite the Tynwald Hill. The name of the road should give us the clue to where we are heading. St Johns was the "Crewe Junction" of the Island — the place where the three separate railway companies met and ultimately interchanged. Eventually all three amalgamated, the Manx Northern Railway and the Foxdale Railway being absorbed by the older Isle of Man Railway.

A short distance down the road, we pass the village shop and the last chance on this walk to stock up with food if you have not brought any with you. Next to the shop you will notice two stone parapet walls each side of the road. Look over the one on the left and you will see the forma-

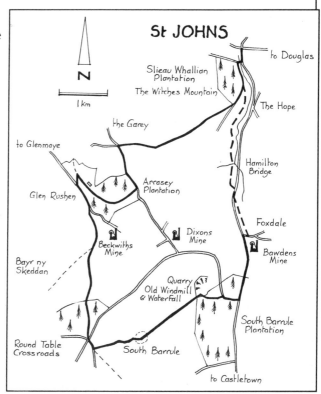

St JOHNS

to Douglas

Slieau Whallian Plantation
The Witches Mountain
The Hope

the Garey

to Glenmaye

Hamilton Bridge

Arrasey Plantation

Glen Rushen

Foxdale

Dixons Mine

Beckwiths Mine

Bawdens Mine

Bayr ny Skeddan

Quarry
Old Windmill & Waterfall

South Barrule Plantation

Round Table Crossroads

South Barrule

to Castletown

1 km

N

tion of the Foxdale Railway rising at a gradient of 1 in 49 to the rear of Pretoria Terrace and curving away to the right to Foxdale two and a half miles away.

Now cross the road (beware of the traffic) and look over the other bridge parapet and, sure enough, it looks more like a railway. There is the old station building dating from 1886, you may be able to make out the line of the platform and you will certainly see the remains of the brick-built water tower.

We next pass an imposing office building which is worth more than a passing look. It was originally the Railway Junction Hotel, one of three hotels built in St Johns to serve the railway which brought so much activity and business to the village. You can imagine its importance in its heyday.

The open area on the left was occupied originally by the Isle of Man Railway and the Manx Northern Railway and was the site of the station, with two platforms and lines with passing loops. There was a galvanised sheet steel-clad carriage shed in the distance on the left, and a signalbox near the stone arch which carried the Foxdale line over the line to Douglas. This whole station area was served by a most unpretentious wooden station building with a small waiting room and station master's office. I can not walk past the area without recalling many happy yarns

about the railway related by Mr Crellin, who was latterly Station Master, sitting in that office surrounded by ticket racks, staffs and oil lamps.

Leaving the railway behind, we turn right at the next junction and cross the Foxdale River over Delaney's Bridge. Look over the bridge to the left — do you see anything vaguely familiar? Well, yes, it looks like a ladder and so it is. One of the footbridges you can see there is made from the bottom section of the 100ft fireman's turntable ladder which was a Dorman Merryweather purchased in 1936 by Douglas Corporation.

Over Delaney's Bridge, we turn left and head uphill under the shadow of Slieau Whallian. Folklore has it that witches were rolled down this hill in spiked barrels. If the person accused of witchcraft was still alive on reaching the bottom she was certainly a witch and the accusers would have no alternative but to slay her. A case of heads I win, tales you lose...

Some distance up the hill, just before the entrance to Slieau Whallian farm, there is an unsurfaced road off to the right, with a sign indicating that it is unsuitable for motors. That's the one that we are going up, through the gate and a steady half-mile climb. The track is an old public road to the Garey and Glen Maye. We shall follow it to the Garey, skirting the eastern flank of Slieau Whallian (1,093ft) all the way. Before we reach the top, the track flattens out a little and it is a good place to take a breather.

The view behind us overlooks the Beary and Greeba, with Colden just visible behind Greeba. Ahead of us is Foxdale, with Stoney Mountain above it and in the far distance, we can see the Mount and Chibbanagh Plantation. The panorama is completed by South Barrule and, just coming into view, Cronk ny Irree Laa.

At the top, the track opens out onto the open moorland and we can look back at the summit of Slieau Whallian. Ahead, we can now see one of the

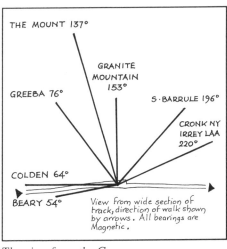

THE MOUNT 137°

GRANITE MOUNTAIN 153°

GREEBA 76°

S·BARRULE 196°

CRONK NY IRREY LAA 220°

COLDEN 64°

BEARY 54°

View from wide section of track, direction of walk shown by arrows. All bearings are Magnetic.

The view from the Garey

(left) IMR Nº 8 Fenella approaching St Johns station with Nº 5 Mona at the rear. The signal box, carriage shed and signals have now been removed.

microwave communication stations, linking the UK to the Island and Eire. The track swings round the southern slopes of the hill and we come to a gated stile. The track disappears, but we continue in a straight line across the field and come to another gate. The track reappears between two solid hedges, soon joining the surfaced road from Glen Maye at the Garey, where we turn left towards Arrasey Plantation.

We climb for a short distance and then the road drops downhill past the transmitter station. Just before we reach the cattle grid, we leave the road and turn right into the plantation. The track is wide and easy to follow and we soon find ourselves among the trees, but only for a short while, before emerging into a clearing with a dramatic view over Glen Rushen or Glion Mooar (the great glen) dominated by South Barrule, one of the ancient hills of watch and ward. Cronk ny Irree Laa completes the picture, with Dalby Mountain just appearing on the right.

The surface remains of Beckwiths Mine can clearly be seen in the foreground. By 1866, the mine was effectively worked out having reached a depth of 185 fathoms but having earned £3/4m from the lead ore produced.

A little further along the track, as we approach the trees again, there is a fork in the track. Keep left on the main track which traverses the hillside below the old farmhouse at Arrasey, an old shieling name and which is now perpetuated in the name of the plantation. Just by the house, the forest has been thinned below the track to open up a superb view of the long disused workings of the Glen Rushen Slate Quarries — much better than the view from the road in the glen over which the old Herring Road (used, as the name suggests, for carrying fish from Peel) passes.

Can you imagine up to 120 men working on the five levels across the valley? The huge spoil heaps at the end of each level consist of the dross and waste from splitting stone to win roofing slates for the Island's building trade. Unfortunately the quality of the slate in this area was not good and the best that could be produced were known as Manx Tun slates. Because of the poor quality of the stone, the slates were heavy and much thicker than imported roofing material. By 1900, the industry had virtually worked itself out but, because of its inaccessibility, the workings and its remains are reasonably intact. The slate vein can be seen running diagonally across the quarry faces virtually the whole height of the mountain.

Continue along the track until we get to an old quarry. We must be careful just as we get to the quarry and take the grassy track to the left, going steeply downhill until we join an old stone wall. We have to turn very sharp left and continue downhill to the Glen Rushen Road, with good views of the glen ahead of

us. At the road, turn left and follow the road up the glen following the route of the Beyr ny Skeddan (Herring Way) almost to
the raw water intake, being careful to take the right fork opposite the reservoir.

At the head of the glen, look out for the green right of way
marker to the left, before the bridge over the river. Following
the bank of the river, we take the old road up the left hand side
of the waterworks. Mind your head as you duck under a cast iron
water pipe and look up the glen on the left: It is named Glion
Corragh, meaning marshy glen — such an unusual name for a
rocky gorge, I wonder where it got its name. It is hard to think
that the road up which we are walking is still a public road. It
served a small community of crofters, typical of many in the
area who depended on the mining industry. These hardy self-
sufficient people left upon the demise of the mines, many making
a new life in the Americas, especially in Ohio and Colorado.
Little remains of their buildings, although old plans show several houses and a chapel hereabouts.

The track is always muddy, even in summer, and it is often
easier to walk on the top of the adjoining Manx "hedge". At the
top of the worst bit, just before the ruined farm, there is a gate.
Stop and look back down the glen. We can see Beckwiths Mine
from the other side now, and the familiar landmark of its chimney leaning at a drunken angle.

The farm, surrounded by its windswept trees, is worth a
look, but remember it is private property and we must respect
that. Imagine what it was like to live here — idyllic in summer,
but hell in winter. Judging by the corner stones, many of which
have been removed, I would guess that the buildings were built
by Cornishmen. Before we leave, just take a look behind the
barn and you will see the remains of a horse mill (*see illustration on page 36*). Many upland farms depended on animal power
to drive their mills, despite the presence of so much running
water. They were resourceful — they had to be.

We continue up the track to the Round Table crossroads,
crossing the road to the stile opposite, leading onto the mountain.
There is a well worn path which we follow to the top of South
Barrule but if it is misty, and you are in doubt, follow a bearing
of 95°. Let's hope it is a lovely clear day because the views from
the top are great. The whole of the south of the Island can be seen,
from Douglas to Ballasalla and Langness, with its lighthouse, and
Castletown with its castle. Port St Mary and Bradda Head, overlooking Port Erin and the Calf of Man, can be seen in the distance.
Looking along the ridge to the right of Bradda, we can make out
successively the Carnanes, then the Sloc and the Burroos, leading
up to Cronk ny Irree Laa, and Cronk Fedjag (hill of the plover), a
little over a mile from where we stand, on South Barrule.

If the weather is good it is an ideal lunch stop, giving us time to take in the view, with Cringle Reservoir in the foreground below us. You will see from the plaque on the top of the hill that we are within the ramparts of an ancient hill fort which encircled a large number of huts. At 1,585ft above sea level, the people who inhabited this hilltop site 500 years BC must have felt very secure, with com-

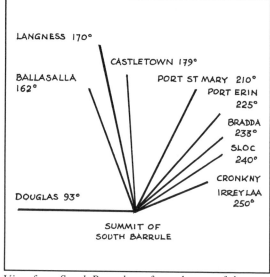

LANGNESS 170°

CASTLETOWN 179°

BALLASALLA 162°

PORT ST MARY 210°

PORT ERIN 225°

BRADDA 233°

SLOC 240°

CRONKNY IRREY LAA 250°

DOUGLAS 93°

SUMMIT OF SOUTH BARRULE

View from South Barrule — from the top of the mountain the whole of the south of the Island can be seen

manding views of the approach from all sides.

Suitably refreshed, we are going to make our way over the open moorland to South Barrule Quarry. We can not see our destination from the summit, so we head off on a bearing of 55°. If you have no compass, look for the summits of Greeba and Slieau Ruy, beyond the Central Valley, and aim for them.

On our way down the broad back of South Barrule we can look across the centre of the Island and the northern hills, with Barrule Beg (little Barrule) below us forming a second summit on Barrule. Just before it lies our destination, the scar of South Barrule Slate Quarries and, if we are on the right heading, we should be aiming for the corner of the plantation and the stone boundary wall. There is a wooden stile at the corner and we cross the fence into the quarry. It is still a working quarry where stone is won for the building industry and road maintenance from the old "deads" and occasionally from a working face.

We follow the boundary wall down to the gate in the bottom corner of the quarry. When the quarry was worked in the latter part of the 19th century, it gave employment to 20 men. Unlike Glen Rushen Quarries, the quality of the slate at Barrule was better with good blue slate, ideal for splitting. There was also a windmill-driven saw used for dressing stone and its remains are there in front of us. Ask the quarry foreman and I am sure he will let you have a closer look.

The remains of the windmill at South Barrule Slate Quarries. It was used for dressing the Manx grey slate from which it also has been constructed.

27

We have seen a number of hidden corners on this walk but the next one is well hidden indeed.

Beyond the gate, we go into the plantation and down the track through the trees alongside Struan Barrule (the Barrule stream) running in the gully on our right. We come into a clearing soon and the track follows the right hand side of the clearing. Half way through the clearing, stop and listen. Can you hear the waterfall?

In winter this small double waterfall can clearly be seen in the moss-covered gorge, with water splashing all over the ferns in its rich dank dark green enclosure. In summer, it is often a trickle, silent as it flows over the moss mat. If you climb down to have a closer look, be careful as the bank if very slippery.

Off we go, down the track, passing another water intake and joining the highway which we follow down to the main Castletown to St Johns road and turn left, walking into Higher Foxdale where, if you have had enough, you can catch a bus back to Douglas.

I'm still game for a bit more walking, so come with me down the Mines Road to the school and follow the old Foxdale Railway track back to St Johns and we shall catch the bus back to Douglas from there.

Ghost town, secluded glen and wild women

3 hours
8 miles

A walk from the fine old port of Peel to look for the site of the Knockaloe internment camp... and for the scene of an historic battle.

THIS walk is centred on Peel and we take the No.6 bus to get there. We get off the bus at the bottom of Station Road outside what used to be Peel Railway Station, opposite the Creek Inn, formerly the Railway Hotel. Many years ago, I spent long hours in "The Railway" talking to Jack Lowney, a long-time driver on the railway and at that time, the regular driver of No.5 *Mona*.

The station building is now a ships' chandlery, the old goods

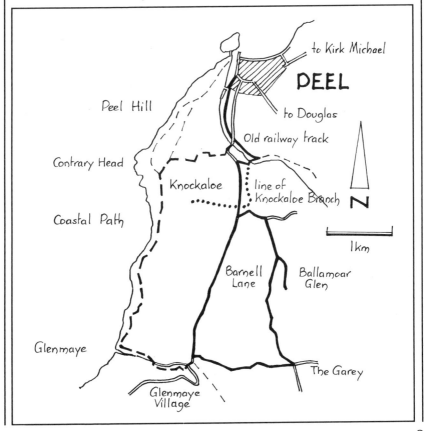

29

shed is the home for the museum housing the Viking longship replica, while the station yard is a boat park.

The railway reached Peel from Douglas in 1873, with the inaugural train arriving on the July 1. Regular services ceased in 1968 and the track was removed five years later. Before we start, let's walk to the harbour's edge and set the mood for the walk by casting our minds back to the first world war. The Isle of Man was chosen by the British Government as a suitable site for the construction of an Alien Detention Camp and Knockaloe Mooar farm, near Peel, was identified as the best site. The camp was built to house 20,000 people, all in timber huts and, in order to facilitate the movement of detainees and troops, a branch line was built to connect the camp with the Peel line and Peel harbour.

A siding was built along the harbour wall from the station yard, eventually connecting the quay to the camp. Imagine the activity, with goods being unloaded and detainees being loaded into coaches for movement. The *Caledonia*, which was the largest and most powerful locomotive, was used exclusively on the branch as far as is known. Having been built for the Foxdale branch of the Manx Northern Railway to handle heavy ore trains, it was ideally suited for the purpose. Once its "cargo" was on board and secured, the train would move off from the station across Mill Road and we shall see where it went.

So off we go along the quay, past the boat park, until we come to the water tank which still stands as yet another memorial to the railway. Turn left into Mill Road and immediately right onto the old track bed which now forms part of the Heritage Rail Trail. Like all good railways, it leaves the town by the back door, through what has always been an industrial area. In 1915, the kipper houses, the mill and a brickworks occupied the site, across the river from a large quarry. Some of these remains can be seen but they are overshadowed by the power station and the Total fuel depot.

Leaving the power station behind, the track bed is more obvious as we run parallel to the old mill race, now used for cooling water for the power station. Alongside is the River Neb, Corrin's Hill is on our right and, ahead of us, Glenfaba House. Soon we come to Glenfaba Bridge which carries the road over the river and, alongside that, the bridge carrying the road over the trackbed. On our left is Glenfaba Mill, complete with water wheel, although the buildings are somewhat dilapidated.

Remember that the scene is centred on the train full of prisoners bound for Knockaloe and a little further on is the place where the branch line forked right. Just before a small footbridge on the old railway trackbed, the formation widens and you can clearly see where the branch left the main line on a facing point leading off to the right on an embankment to the River Neb, which it crossed by a timber bridge.

Carry on along the line towards Douglas, through the cutting, and look for the gate on the right which takes us across the sluice to the Glenfaba Mill and to the main river bank. We go right through a public tree-planting area to the footbridge over the Neb. This bridge is built on the abutments of the old railway bridge and you can easily make out the line of the embankment on each side. That is about all we can see of the line, unfortunately, but if you stop on the footbridge, you can imagine how the line made its way steeply up the field ahead of us towards the camp.

We can not follow the formation as it is on private land, so we turn right and follow the path to the main road, where we turn left and walk towards Patrick Village. The house we pass on the opposite side of the road is The Raggatt and, as we pass it, the land opens out to reveal the broad flat fields of Knockaloe, which was the site of the internment camp. The land is now owned by the Isle of Man Government and is run as an experimental farm for evaluating crops and breeds of animal best suited to Island conditions.

The branch line serving the camp ran parallel to the road on our left. Was the long building running alongside the road and now a bungalow, the old laundry perhaps? The railway ran behind where the bungalows are now built and, in a dramatic curve, crossed the road opposite the farm street to run up the left hand side of it, past the guardhouse, as far as the present farm buildings, which were administration offices for the camp.

The line was built in 1915 and used until 1920, the track being lifted some years later. The gradient of the line was 1 in 20 and Caledonia must have presented an imposing sight as it propelled the train up to the camp. Information on the operation of the branch line is scarce but some photographs of it in use survive in the Manx Museum archives. Nothing remains of the camp but distant memories, the official records, and a few poignant exhibits in the museum at Peel. A ghost town which once housed 20,000 inhabitants.

We continue past the farm to the junction in the centre of the village, and turn left to pass the church, refurbished in 1958, the most recent of several places of worship which have occupied the site. Have a look at the window above the porch, which depicts St Patrick surrounded by the serpents. The churchyard still has graves from the period we have been contemplating, and several military personnel who died at Knockaloe are buried at Patrick. There were also, until recently, graves of internees who died at the camp, but they were repatriated and no record exists now — not even a commemorative plaque.

Returning to the road, we cross the stream on the road bridge, built on the site of Droghad y Chaggey Fuiltagh (the bridge of the bloody battle) where, in 1098 AD, there was a battle between the two tribes who inhabited the north and the south of the Island. It is recorded in the *Chronicles of Man and the Isles* as the Battle of Santwat. There were many losses on both sides and the battle was only won when the women of the north came to the aid of their menfolk and swayed the battle in their favour.

After the bridge, carry on along the road but look out for the first road on the right, which is Barnell Lane (Bayr 'n ell) which means "road of the fell". We walk up it to the point where the surface, such as it is, stops and it becomes rocky. There is a gate on the left and a notice giving permission from the owners, Mr and Mrs Anderson, of Ballamoar, to walk into the Ballamoar Glen. As we go through the gate, be careful to take the lower of the two tracks. This is our hidden corner and beautiful it is at any time of the year. We shall walk as far as the old reservoir which used to serve the town of Peel but is now a conservation area. We can see how beautiful it is from the gate, particularly now that nature is taking over.

We have to return to the gate on Barnell Lane and go left, up the rocky track up the hill. The original name of the road here is Creggan ny Mraane, meaning "the rocky place of the women", and it is supposedly where the women came to the help of their menfolk in the battle of Santwat. Did they hide in ambush? Did the fight extend to the glen? History does not tell us.

We continue uphill, steadily climbing to the Garey and, as the road levels out near the top, we have a view over Slieau Whallian to the left and, if we pause and look behind us, we have a wonderful view of Peel and the west of the Island.

At the Garey, we join a surfaced road which we take to the right and soon start to descend to Glen Maye (the yellow glen), which we can see as a distinct notch in the coastline. With a bit of ingenuity, you can link up with Walk 2, from the Garey, and make a full day's excursion. Otherwise, you will soon find yourself at the main road at Glen Maye, near the village shop.

We turn right and walk back along the road to Patrick, to retrace our steps to Peel and the bus back to Douglas.

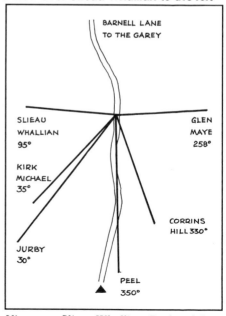

View over Slieau Whallian, Peel and the west

The Buggane, cirques and glacial valleys

5 hours
10 miles

A walk from the Island's central valley, through the hills, almost to the west coast.

A solitary pool at the head of Glen Kiark looks out over the coast and Glen Wyllin. See page 39.

I'M afraid it's the No.6 bus again from Douglas, this time as far as the Highlander, a mile or so beyond Crosby. We get off the bus opposite the Highlander and cross the road to go left to the entrance to King's Forest (or Greeba Plantation) on Greeba Mountain. As you cross the road, look for the church without a roof sitting in the middle of the field. This is St Trinian's, built on the site of a much earlier keeill (chapel). Folklore has it that a roof could not be kept on the church. Every time one was put on, a "phynnodderee", known as the Buggane, would come down off Greeba in a violent storm and blow the roof off.

Passing the Highlander and walking on the pavement, look for

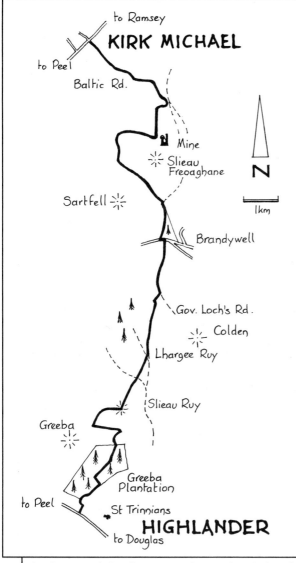

to Ramsey

KIRK MICHAEL

to Peel

Baltic Rd.

Mine

Slieau Freoaghane

N

1km

Sartfell

Brandywell

Gov. Loch's Rd.

Colden

Lhargee Ruy

Slieau Ruy

Greeba

Greeba Plantation

to Peel

St Trinnians

HIGHLANDER

to Douglas

the private entrance gate immediately before the first house we come to. This is the new way into the forest, with its wide road curving up the hill. We must climb over the gate and walk up the new road as far as the old entrance to the King's Forest Plantation, which, as the sign proudly states, is 154 acres in extent and was established in 1906. After about 200 metres on the track, we come to a small clearing in the forest, with a ruined building on the left. Here we are faced with a choice.

You've guessed it — we go left up the very steep grassy track, through the heart of the forest and the home of the Buggane. It is a hard slog for the next quarter of a mile. Half way up, we get a brief respite and the track levels out a little, but it is only shortlived and we are soon climbing again, albeit a little less steeply.

Just as we start to climb again, pause and look back. There is a commanding view of South Barrule framed by the trees of the King's Forest. If the light is right, this is surely worth a picture for anyone with their camera to hand. We eventually come to a fork in the track and again it is left and uphill for a short distance, before the track suddenly swings left and opens up. Now we are at the top, with the gate in the boundary wall straight ahead of us. Sidestep a recently erected fence, climb over the gate and enter the mountain moorland.

Ahead of us is the cirque between Greeba and Slieau Ruy. What is a cirque? Well, it is a bowl-like amphitheatre left when the ice retreated at the end of the last Ice Age. It would have been carved by a glacier, eating back into an area of high land. "Cirque" comes from French, but the words "cwm" and "corrie" are also used, coming from Welsh and Scots Gaelic, respectively. This cirque drains through Bawshen, or Boshen, and, eventually, to Braid ny Boshen (meaning the gorge of the torrent). As with so many Manx place names, the literal translation tells us a lot about its history.

We are heading for the saddle between the two hills, crossing the centre of the cirque and taking the zigzag road right and left to the top. Don't be surprised if we raise a pheasant or two here — and we are bound to be watched from a distance by the odd hare, sitting on his hind legs, checking that we do not get too close to his territory.

As we enter the cirque, we will see it commands, to our right, a view over Marown and Braddan, with Douglas Head and the harbour clearly visible, and the urban sprawl of Douglas and Onchan intruding ever further into the countryside. Crossing the centre of the cirque in winter, you can see water gushing and bubbling its way out of the ground in numerous springs, eventually becoming a tributary of the River Dhoo. Swinging round the zigzag of the path, our views are now of South Barrule, on the left, and the south of the Island, with Langness in the distance. Quite lovely: Slieau Chiarn and the Mount complete the vista.

The track on which we are walking is one of many old bridleways which escaped the attention of James Hamilton, the 18th century Supervisor-General for Highways, but which are nevertheless still well defined, if no longer in general use. Some were roads to the turbaries, used by people exercising their right to dig peat, some were church roads, and some were created by the Commissioners appointed under the terms of the 1860 Disafforesting Act. I'm afraid I have never been able to fully work out the origins of this one, although you can follow it most of the way to Peel.

After an hour's steady climbing from the bus, we should reach the crest of the saddle as Peel and Corrin's Hill come into view. Now we must turn right, heading off on a bearing of 50° towards Slieau Ruy. Looking back, you will see the cairn on Greeba, as we walk the broad back of Greeba, from which we can see Peel on the west

The remains of a horse mill at a deserted farm in Glen Rushen (Walk № 2)

*Ballamoar Glen: hidden place on walk Nº 3,
from Peel*

coast, Castletown in the south, Douglas in the east, and the sea almost all around us.

We circle round the crest of the cirque until the cairn on Slieau Ruy comes into view, being careful to keep on top of the ridge. If the mist comes down, keep on the original bearing until you start to descend, then stop and take a bearing of 90°, being careful to maintain height, and you should come to the top of Slieau Ruy,

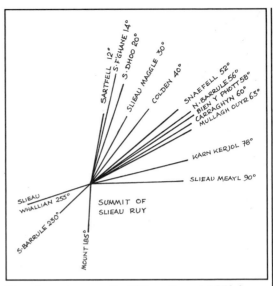

View from the summit of Slieau Ruy at 1,570 ft

meaning "red mountain". It is one of many so called and takes its name from the heather.

The summit of Slieau Ruy is 1,570 ft above sea level and the view from it is, I think, stunning. My wife Carol and I often walk here of a summer's evening from our home in Glenvine. I have even run up here in winter in the light of a full moon and that really is the best way to see this view. No, I'm not locked up yet; I am here with you to admire the view of the Island, with Sartfell, Slieau Freoaghane, Slieau Dhoo, Slieau Maggle, Lhargee Ruy, Colden, Snaefell, North Barrule, Bien-y-Phott, Carraghyn, The Creg, Mullagh Ouyr, Karn Kerjol, Slieau Meayl and Banks Howe spread before us — and that is without turning round behind to look at the southern hills.

We now follow a more defined track down Slieau Ruy to Lhargee Ruy (47°) where we pick up a well-defined track which we follow to the Brandywell road, the last portion of which is over Governor Loch's road, recently widened to service the additional forestry being established on these hills.

From the Brandywell, we cross the road on a staggered left, then right, to go up the track almost opposite, alongside the boundary of the Sartfell Plantation, following the stone boundary wall until it and the track turns to the right and levels off. We are not following the track which leads to Ballaugh; we are striking off straight ahead between the saddle of Sartfell and Slieau Freoaghane (the meaning of which is obscure but is, popularly, "the hill of the bilberry").

Although the way we are taking is obscure, there is a poorly defined track underfoot and, as we breast the saddle, a view of the west coast opens before us and we leave the heather behind. Now the shape of the track, long disused, is more distinct, as it passes a ruined farm. Just below the farm, let's leave the track and scramble down the bank by some old workings to find a small pool, always covered in a green water plant, not unlike watercress, and with rushes at the edge.

This is our first hidden corner where we can sit and admire the view, having earned a break. See the deep gorge of Glen Wyllin cutting the profile of the coast. Imagine the force of water that cut the glen and, nearer us, the valley of Cooil Dharry, which we shall look at more closely on our next walk. Where did all that water come from? Well, the answer lay in the ice sheet as it retreated and lingered in this valley and the next. We are at the head of Glen Kiark (the name relates to moorhens) and the water collects from here and runs eventually through Cooil Dharry.

Now we go back up to the track and follow it down the southern flank of Slieau Freoaghane, keeping the hill on our right all the time. The views from the track now extend to Ballaugh and Jurby, where we can see the white outline of Jurby Parish Church standing on Jurby Head.

The path becomes more difficult to follow but it still forms a ledge on the side of Slieau Freoaghane, coming close to the mountain boundary wall. As we round the corner, we emerge above a reservoir and join a more defined track and suddenly, ahead of us, is the second hidden place. The impressive glacial valley nestling between Slieau Freoaghane and Slieau Dhoo is always dramatic, winter or summer (*see illustration on page 40*).

The track leads on up the floor of the valley to the ruined workings of the Kirk Michael mine, which recalls another attempt to find the same productive vein of galena which yielded rich supplies of lead at Laxey, on the opposite coast. Like so many of these small trials, it was unproductive and soon abandoned. We continue to the mine buildings and then cross the river by the path below the spoil heap.

Look across the valley and you will see a steep path ahead, almost like an incline for the mine, which it may well have been, running straight up the side of the hill. You've guessed it — that is the way we are going! It is a good stiff climb, but the views are superb.

At the top, the track levels off and again and is difficult to follow. Keep going in the same general direction over the open moorland and, after about a quarter of a mile, we shall join a track which comes up from Kirk Michael village. Turn left and

The glacial valley that nestles between Slieau Freoaghane and Slieu Dhoo

follow it downhill, first as a grassy track and then as a rough track until the first house and signs of civilisation, after which the road is surfaced.

Kirk Michael is spread beneath us and we continue down the road, known locally as the Baltic Road, to the centre of the village, where we shall catch the bus and return to Douglas.

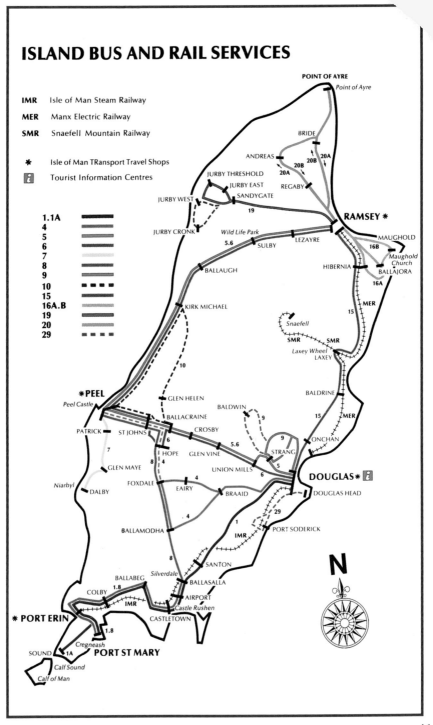

ISLAND BUS AND RAIL SERVICES

IMR   Isle of Man Steam Railway

MER   Manx Electric Railway

SMR   Snaefell Mountain Railway

✳   Isle of Man TRansport Travel Shops

ℹ️   Tourist Information Centres

1.1A
4
5
6
7
8
9
10
15
16A.B
19
20
29

POINT OF AYRE

Point of Ayre

BRIDE

ANDREAS   20B   20A

20A   20B

JURBY THRESHOLD

JURBY EAST

SANDYGATE

REGABY

JURBY WEST

19

RAMSEY ✳

MAUGHOLD

JURBY CRONK

Wild Life Park

5.6   SULBY   LEZAYRE

16B

Maughold Church

BALLAUGH

HIBERNIA   BALLAJORA

16A

KIRK MICHAEL

Snaefell

SMR   SMR

Laxey Wheel   LAXEY

MER

15

10

✳PEEL

Peel Castle

GLEN HELEN

BALDWIN

BALDRINE

BALLACRAINE

9

PATRICK   ST JOHNS   CROSBY

15   MER

7

6

HOPE

GLEN VINE

5.6

9

ONCHAN

8   4

STRANG

GLEN MAYE

UNION MILLS

5

Niarbyl   DALBY

FOXDALE   EAIRY

6

DOUGLAS ✳ ℹ️

4

BRAAID

DOUGLAS HEAD

4

29

BALLAMODHA

1

PORT SODERICK

IMR

8

SANTON

Silverdale

BALLABEG   BALLASALLA

COLBY   1.8

AIRPORT

IMR

Castle Rushen

✳ PORT ERIN   CASTLETOWN

1.8

SOUND   1A

Cregneash

PORT ST MARY

Calf Sound

Calf of Man

N

41

The elusive valley

5 ½hours
10 miles

A walk recalling the heyday of the old Manx Northern Railway and visiting the site of a Tynwald court held nearly 600 years ago.

THIS walk is in the true spirit of the RailTrail series. Take the No.6 bus again, to Peel, and get off at the Town Hall, opposite the parish church of St German. The church is worth more than a passing glance, so let us walk through the grounds. Now the Cathedral of Mann, the church was built in 1884 in the style of the early English. Its exposed position above the old town resulted in the roof being severely damaged in a

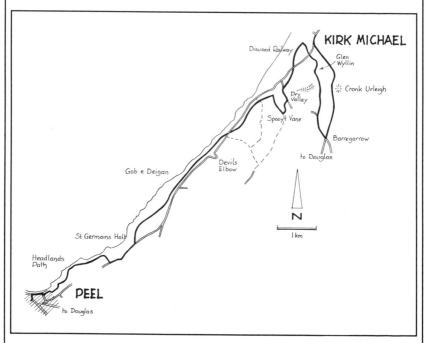

storm in 1903 and again, in 1907, another storm damaged the spire atop the tower. As we walk down through the grounds to the main gates in Athol Street, you will see, on the left, some of the masonry from the spire, which was demolished following the storm.

Turn right along Athol Street and down Bridge Street to the Promenade. Once there, we turn right and start the walk proper towards the tall sandstone buildings at the far end of the Promenade. Look for Walpole Road and head up it to the lane on the left, to the rear of the houses. At the lane, look for the concrete-surfaced pathway, leading over the grassy headland, and follow it round to the cliff above the end of the Promenade. A pause here to look back at Peel gives us a classic view of the town, nestled under Peel Hill, with the parish church standing guard at one end and, Peel Castle at the other.

We now join the headlands path, which forms part of the Island's Coastal Footpath, and walk generally northwards, with views towards the White Strand and Kirk Michael, the sandy coastline leading up to Jurby Head in the far distance.

The first point of interest is Traie Fagog (Periwinkle Shore) and the entrance to the old swimming baths which can clearly be seen, as can the remains of the old open-air pool. We shall soon leave the more recent development of Peel behind and appreciate the wild nature of the coastline and the profusion of birdlife which inhabits this section of coast.

The large rocky outcrop, which is fairly obvious and on our left, half way along the path, is known as the Stack, and if you look carefully you will see where the tops of caves have collapsed either side of it. In some cases, further collapsing has left holes through which you can hear the waves breaking, particularly on a stormy day.

A little further along, the path takes a bit of a dogleg inland at a promontory known as Lhoob y Rheast (Gully of the Moor). If you stop here and look along the stony shoreline, it is usually full of gulls.

The path continues above it and is clearly defined and, in summer, often shoulder-high with bracken on both sides. Soon we emerge above Cass Struan (meaning stream-end), with Cain's Strand round the next headland and the smooth wave-washed sandstone cliffs between. Here we follow the path inland, down some rough-cut steps, to join the main coast road from Peel to Kirk Michael.

Turn left at the road and follow it for about quarter of a mile, taking care where there are no pavements. At the top of the hill, look out for the Coastal Path signs leading left past what looks like an old railway station.

Sure enough, it was originally St German's Halt, built by the Manx Northern Railway in 1879 to serve Peel. The Manx Northern was built to connect the north of the Island and its principal town of Ramsey to the Isle of Man Railway at St Johns, which already connected Douglas to the west and the south. You could even buy a ticket here to Whitehaven or Belfast, but if you had come from Peel, you would have had either a brisk walk or a rough ride in a horse-drawn carriage.

Nothing much remains of the railway now, since the line was removed in 1973, other than some of the buildings and the fine masonry bridges which were built by J & W Grainger, of Glasgow, contractor to the original railway company, later absorbed by the Isle of Man Railway.

We are going to walk along the section of line which was, without doubt, the most dramatic and scenic of all the Island's railways. I can clearly remember the thrill of riding along this section of line, bound for Glen Wyllin on Sunday School picnics, when all you seemed to see was sea and sky, and then you appeared to fly as you crossed the big glens on high viaducts. These were young memories. My most recent memories were of riding on the diesel railcars which, with their bus-type bodies, offered a much wider view all round. Enough of that, we are here to walk...

The line starts sedately enough as we curve out towards the coast again, and the sleeper indentations can clearly be seen as we stagger across them. It is only for a short distance and we soon emerge below Knocksharry, crossing Glen Brooigh (the dirty glen). The embankment is only short, but high, although most of it is obscured by the abundant tree growth on both sides. The stream which drains the boggy area at Lhergy Colvine, on the hills above us on the right, drains down onto the shore at Ballanayre Strand on our left.

Ahead of us, on the skyline and slightly to our left, we can just make out the cutting where the line emerges onto the cliff face above Gob e Deighan. As we continue along the track bed, we swing under a bridge which carries the road leading down to the shore at Gob e Deighan (the meaning of this name is obscure, but is thought to relate to a ship which was wrecked here long ago). Folklore tells a tale of a merman, half man, half fish, who frequents this place. I have not seen him yet but I am still looking.

We could, if you want to, climb out of the cutting near the bridge abutment and follow the path to the beach, where, if the weather is good and the tide is out, we can explore the caves at the southern edge of the bay. There are hidden corners here and maybe that is where the merman is hiding! If the weather is too good then we might get no further and end up soaking in the sun for the rest of the day...

Perhaps we had better stay on the old railway line which continues here in a deep cutting (the one we could see in the distance), then suddenly we emerge on the side of a cliff above the shore. This was so dramatic from the train because one minute all you could see was the grass on the embankment and then, the open sea and sky. What you could not see was that the track was on an embankment on the cliff and this gave the railway endless trouble with settlement, as can still be seen now as we walk along.

We pass the old platelayers' hut and find ourselves on a boggy section of the trackbed for a short distance, passing Lower Ballakaighen Farm before crossing the second glen on an embankment. This is Glion Cam (the twisting glen). Above us to our right, the coast road negotiates the head of the glen at the aptly named Devil's Elbow. This section of road was used for the first TT motorcycle races between 1907 and 1911, before the event was moved to the now world-famous route through the mountains.

IMR Nº 5 Mona with a Ramsey train crossing Glen Mooar Viaduct

Below us, the stream meanders to the sea at Lady Port, which roughly marks the point at which the coastline changes from rock to sand and, from now onwards north to the Point of Ayre, the coast is subject to sea erosion.

The track swings under the coast road by the Jubilee Bridge at Skerestal (rocky farm). Just after the skew bridge we find ourselves in a rock cutting and it is worth looking at the rock formation with its quartz veins.

We continue past Ballaquine Farm on high ground, commanding views northward, with Kirk Michael in the distance. Where the railway crossed the road leading to Ballacamane, the girders have been removed. We just follow the right of way down one side of the abutment and up the other. Look at the engineering bricks which form the coping to the abutment. The manufacturer's name, JJ Wood, of West Bromwich, is proudly displayed on one of the bricks. I wonder if the brickworks is still there?

Back on the track bed again, we can very clearly see below us the cliff erosion I mentioned, and in time I suspect the coast road itself will be threatened.

Now we are at the third glen that the railway crossed, only this time on high lattice girders, supported on masonry piers. The girders are no longer there, but the piers are. We must go into Glen Mooar (the big glen) down the path, turning right under the first pier. The piers are worth more than a passing glance. They were built in the winter of 1878/9 when there were no sophisticated tower cranes or modern lifting gear to help the builders — they just had wooden scaffold and block and tackle. Look at the size of the stone blocks in the centre of the piers, and the detail on the sandstone corner stones — craftsmen indeed.

We follow the main path up the glen, which is beautiful in summer and autumn with many decorative shrubs interspersed with mature trees. As we start to climb up to the head of the glen, we suddenly find ourselves in an opening among the trees and below us are the remains of Cabbal Pharic (St Patrick's Chapel). If we stop and listen, we can probably hear a waterfall and, as we continue along the path, it will certainly get louder. This is our hidden corner and we must be careful not to miss the path leading off to the left, to Spooyt Vane (the white spout) where I suggest we stop near the foot of the waterfall for lunch.

After our lunch stop, it's back up the steps to the main path for a short distance, crossing the footbridge above the head of the waterfall and going along the track until we join the Ballaleigh Road, near the disused Spooyt Vane chapel.

We head off down the road to rejoin the railway at the former level crossing. Be careful not to miss it: the clue is in the gatekeeper's house, now much modified, where we turn to the right onto the old railway trackbed. Just before we get to the old crossing, there is a sharp bend in the road before the bungalow on the right. There is a gate on the corner where I want to stop and look inland over Ballaleigh. Can you see, in the distance, what looks like a rocky gorge? It is a classic dry river valley — perhaps the best example on the Island, but quite inaccessible.

Just remember it for the moment, as I shall refer to it later. Meanwhile, back on the track, the cutting is deep here, and curves gently under the road bridge. The banks of the cutting between the two road bridges enjoy a profusion of wild flowers, perhaps the best to be found anywhere on the Island. As we approach the second bridge, let your mind wander back in time and imagine one of the Manx Northern Sharp Stewart 2-4-0 tank engines rattling round the curve with a rake of Clemison six-wheeled carriages resplendent in varnished teak — what a sight!

Back to reality, we must press on a little further until we come to the abutment of the second major viaduct which crossed the fourth glen on this section of the railway. Glen Wyllin, meaning the mill glen, was owned by the railway company and filled with entertainments for all ages. Bowls, tennis, swings, slides, roundabouts, a boating lake and a café. It was the destination for those Sunday school picnics I mentioned earlier. The railway crossed the glen on high plate girders, carried on tall masonry piers, as it approached Kirk Michael Station, which was the stop for Glen Wyllin.

The girders are no longer in place, so we have to walk down the side of the glen, now used as a campsite and still giving pleasure to many people. Turn right at the bottom of the embankment and walk up the glen to the main coast road. Notice the flat grassy areas on the right where the bowling greens and tennis courts used to be.

When we reach the main road, cross straight over and go up the narrow road ahead. We are now in the village of Glen Wyllin proper, almost a hidden place in itself. Most people rush by on the main road and do not know it exists. Carry on until we come to the mill after which the glen is named. Look for the unsurfaced track to the right of the mill and walk up it, beneath the trees. This is the Cooil Dharry road and, believe it or not, it is a public road. As we climb uphill, we are between high hedges, but as it levels out, we are rewarded with views over the western hills.

There is a little dip in the road here and a small disused quarry on the right. The dip is where one of the two main rivers which carved glen Mooar used to run, but there is no river there now. I asked you to remember the distant view of the gorge — well, this is the top of it and the river rushed down towards the sea on the right, carving its way through Ballaleigh and Glen Mooar.

Where is the river now? Well, it is now a tributary of the river which carved Glen Wyllin and about 180 feet below us on the left. It starts at Glen Kiark, on the side of Slieau Freoaghane and in the glacial valley, both described in Walk No. 4. The old watercourse to our right is now left as a dry river, with steep walls of rock on both sides.

How can this be? It is a common enough phenomenon in areas where glacial activity has taken place, but not so easy to see here. This particular dry river valley is quite difficult to understand, as the head of the Glen Wyllin valley is considered to be preglacial. The theory is that the Glen Wyllin below us on the left, remained full of ice as the ice sheet gradually thawed and the run-off from the glacier came the shortest route from Glion Kiark, straight across the ice in the valley, scoured out the valley at Ballaleigh, and then carried on to Glen Mooar. As the melt continued and the level of the ice dropped in the Glen Wyllin gorge, so the water took the easy route and ran into Glen Wyllin, leaving the dry river valley with no catchment. As Michael Caine would say, "Not many people know that!"

While looking over the hedge towards Glen Kiark and Slieau Freoaghane, can you see Cronk Urleigh or Reneurling? It is the prominent grass-covered earth mound just above the main road. The meaning of its name appears confused and obscure. It is almost certainly a morainic deposit, left behind by the melting ice. One thing however is absolutely certain — a Tynwald Court was held on the hill in 1422, at which a number of local people were accused of treason, among other things. All of this is documented in the written Statutes of the Isle of Man — and all of this 76 years before Columbus reached America.

This rather insignificant looking mound of glacial gravel and drift, the surrounding hills, the gorge below and the dry valley behind are all that is left to bear testimony to secrets kept hidden for centuries.

We carry on up the Cooil Dharry road until we join the Ballaleigh Road and go straight on to Barregarrow crossroads. Admire the view of the western hills as we approach Barregarrow, it's probably the best view of the hills we shall get.

Cross the road at Barregarrow, turn left and follow the footway alongside the road all the way to Kirk Michael for our return to Douglas by bus. We are following the TT Course: can you imagine riding a motorcycle through here at more than 140mph. Which reminds me, if walking in June or September, the roads will be closed for racing at certain times and you will have to turn right when you join the Ballaleigh Road and walk back to the coast road. If time is short before your bus, you may have to choose this option anyway, as it is shorter.

A winter view on Walk Nº 4 looking towards Peel from the source of the river Neb. Cronk ny Irrey Laa is in the far distance.

|||||| (Above) The rocky gorge near Ballaleigh which is described in Walk Nº 5.
Now a dry river valley, it is seen here from the "gate on the corner".
(Below) Our objective in Walk Nº 6: Creg Bedn on the top of Slieau
Managh, or Carrick y Chiyt to give it its other name

IMR Nº 15 Caledonia charging a snowdrift at Ellenbrook on the climb out of Douglas, 5th March 1965. The Caledonia, being the most powerful locomotive on the Island, was brought out of retirement when snow brought the winter service to a halt. However, no driver remained who could handle the old engine. Retired senior driver, Arthur Cain (inset), was asked back to help clear the snows, along with the regular crew Jim Cowell and John Elkin (left), now the senior driver.

The wild cats of Ohio

**5 hours
10 miles**

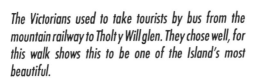

The Victorians used to take tourists by bus from the mountain railway to Tholt y Will glen. They chose well, for this walk shows this to be one of the Island's most beautiful.

THIS is a circular walk, based on Sulby Village. Unfortunately, the train no longer runs to Sulby so it is the No.5 bus to Ramsey via Kirk Michael, but remember to get off at Sulby Village. The bus ride itself is worth every penny, particularly between Peel and Kirk Michael as it closely follows the route of the railway, which can be clearly seen from the bus, from St German's Halt to Kirk Michael (see Walk No.5).

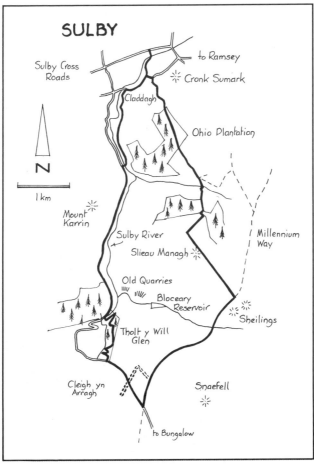

The view over Jane's House, on the Calf of Man, (Walk Nº 14) looking up the west coast of the Isle of Man. The Sound and Thousla rock are in the foreground, Kitterland and the Little Sound behind that and Port Erin and Bradda Head in the distance.

We should make sure we have food with us, although there are good opportunities to eat at the Tholt-y-Will Hotel and in Sulby Village itself.

So, from the bus stop we cross the road and look for the right of way sign beside the Glen Kella whisky distillery. The building was originally a woollen mill, operated by the Penrice family and before that, the Southward family. The path crosses the Sulby River and the old weir to the dam, and then follows the bank of the river to the Claddagh Road, which we join and follow to the left as far as the bridge at Ballamenagh. Be careful here — we are going straight on, following the right bank of the stream, along the Old Dock Road (don't ask me why it has this name: I don't know).

A short distance after the Ballamenagh farm buildings, the road turns sharp right. We are going slightly left, over a stile following the right of way sign. Cross the stream and head off up the track, where we cross two more stiles before entering Ohio Plantation. If you look back you can see the distinctive shape of Cronk Sumark and Ballamenagh House and, in the distance, Jurby Church.

It is a steady plod for almost 20 minutes up through the plantation. Look out for the fungi growing on banks beside the track, they seem to thrive here all year round. At the top we emerge through a gate and follow a distinct track between the upland pastures. I well remember discovering that many of these fields were part of farms in Andreas and Lezayre and used as summer grazing.

Follow the track for about quarter of a mile and then look for a waymarker by the bend in the track, with a dilapidated wall each side. Just on the right there is a stile over the post-and-wire fence. Hop over and cross the field diagonally to the next way marker and stile. You will notice that we are now on a wide track, which we follow to the Clugget River. This is the old road which gave access to Slieau Managh (the Monk's Mountain), which is where we are heading.

I have written this description three times now and each time walked the route and tried to put myself in the position of a stranger. It is really quite difficult to follow the established right of way, so do be careful — use the map. This has long been a favourite walk and I first walked it before the plantation was formed. Now the numerous fences make the going difficult.

Cross the river and follow the track towards the gate, but do not go through it; swing right and continue uphill alongside the gully, keeping the stone wall on your left. At the head of the gully there is a substantial stone wall which is the old mountain boundary wall, which you must climb as best you can. Now, on your right, there is a post-and-wire fence with a stile. Cross it and go into the plantation and there is an unplanted firebreak which is quite wide. Follow that uphill to the next post-and-wire fence about 200 yards away. There is a fixed gate in the fence which is easy to cross. We are heading for the big lump of rock on the side of Slieau Managh, which is our hidden place.

Once you know where to look, you can see it for miles. However, if the cloud is down, you will not see it, even from here, in which case, having crossed the the last fence, turn right and follow it for a short distance until another fence joins it from the left. There is another fixed gate which you cross to gain the open moorland. If you can see the Creg Bedn (the name translates as White Rock) then head straight for it. If not, take a bearing of 220° from the gate and follow that.

This is our hidden place — almost on top of a hill, just to be different...

The Creg Bedn is a glaciated crag of vein quartz almost five metres high and 20 metres long. From a geological point of view, it provides good indications that glacial movement in this area was uphill, and adds to the supportive evidence that the Island was entirely covered by an ice sheet during the last Ice Age. Anyway, it is a substantial piece of white quartz and well named.

It is a good viewpoint so let us have a rest and admire the view. The rock also has another name, not perhaps so well known and certainly not as obvious. It is Carrick y chiyt (rock of the cat), perhaps a reference to the presence of wild cats hereabouts in the past, or the polecat maybe? Either way, I have not seen any up here yet, but I am still looking.

Having admired the view from the rock, we should use our compass and set a bearing of 140°, over Slieau Managh, heading for the cairn on the Millennium Way. Even on a clear day, it is easier to use the

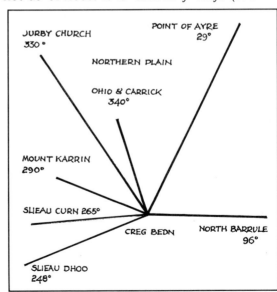

The view from Creg Bedn

compass. If you have not got one, keep slightly left of the summit of Slieau Managh, and as the distant hills become visible, head for Clagh Ouyr on the skyline and you will reach the Millennium Way.

Turn right at the cairn and follow the waymarkers down past the shielings, which are the circular mounds on our left as we drop down to the Bloc Eairy stream. These shielings are yet another, even older, visible record of transhumance — the seasonal movement of livestock between mountain and lowland pasture. The young men looked after the sheep on the hills and sheltered in these circular depressions, covered with bracken or cloth against the rain. Not for them the luxury of four-wheel drive vehicles.

You may have noticed on our right on the way down, a reservoir at Bloc Eairy: it is fed by the stream which we have to cross.

We are now standing under the massive bulk of Snaefell, the Island's highest mountain, and we must pick our way through a very wet section and climb straight up and over the western flank. It is fairly well defined and waymarked and we should have no problem following it round to meet a stone boundary wall and a very substantial earth mound, which is part of an ancient earthwork known as Cleigh yn Arragh. The literal interpretation means "rampart of turf and stones" and as that adequately describes what we see, it will certainly do for me.

As we walk alongside this earthwork, we can see the distinctive shape of Beinn y Phott ahead of us. When we reach the Tholt y Will Road, we leave the Millennium Way and turn right, following the road downhill, crossing the Cleigh yn Arragh again by the cattle grid.

A little further down the road, we come to the top wall of the Tholt y Will glen, now one of the Island's many National Glens. Originally, the glen was owned by the Manx Electric Railway, from 1907, with a charabanc service connecting the glen to the Bungalow halt on the Snaefell Mountain Railway. The service was first operated by two Argus vehicles which were converted to lorries in the winter and carried cross open-bench seats in the summer. The service did not continue after the second world war, which also saw the tramway company's involvement in the glen come to an end. The glen came into Government ownership when the tramway was nationalised in 1957 and it was transferred to what was then the Forestry Board, becoming a National Glen.

We shall sample the simple pleasures of a Victorian Glen. Follow the path into the glen and zigzag down through the trees, taking time to admire the views through the trees and into the

The upper reaches of the Silverburn river at Grenaby on Walk Nº 10

lower reaches of the Sulby valley. Eventually, we come to a latch gate. Do not go through it, but instead turn right just before it and follow the path down some moss-covered concrete steps which can be quite slippery. Then cross a gorge by a wooden bridge and here is yet another hidden corner — the Alt Waterfall — always damp, always green, sometimes misty, often eerie. Yes, the Victorians knew a thing or two about the beauty of nature and the Manx knew a thing or two about the "lil people".

Continue along the path, skirting the very top of the glen, soon descending some steep steps which command spectacular views through the trees, almost to the bottom of the valley. The path continues until it joins an old roadway leading to the ruined tholtan (farmstead) we can just see above us. Following the grassy road downhill, until we come to a left hand hairpin, where it really starts to drop. Resist the temptation and cross through the broken gap in the stone wall straight ahead of us to follow the old pathways through the loveliest part of the glen. Soon the path starts to descend by some steps and you can see a wooden footbridge below. Be careful and look for the path leading off to the right. It is hard to see but it runs uphill a short way and crosses a stream by yet another footbridge. Now follow the path right to the end of the glen until the way is barred by a fallen tree. The path drops down almost to the Sulby River which we then follow back upstream, crossing the bridge we saw earlier from the top of the glen, and yet another bridge across the main river, to emerge by the Celtic Craft Centre with the Tholt y Will Hotel nearby... certainly a good place for a break and some refreshment before continuing down the glen.

Suitably refreshed, we walk down the road towards Sulby, passing on our right the remains of the quarrying activity in the Bloc Eary area. Although it is much changed now by the presence of pipework to the small hydro-electric generator in the stone building, you can still just make out the levels and inclines in connection with the quarrying which was centred a little further up the valley, where some more surface remains can be seen. Two adits were driven in the valley to search for a continuation of the Laxey ore, a vein similar to that of the Snaefell Mine. Despite driving for 100 fathoms (a little over 190 metres) nothing of any value was found. The slate from the quarries was mostly used for building.

There are few buildings in the valley, which is really the most beautiful in the Island, differing greatly with the moods of the seasons, from the bluebells in spring to the russet of the bracken in autumn. In the middle of winter, the streams you can see trickling down the sides of the valley become raging torrents of wild white water.

A little under two miles down the valley, look out for a right of way sign leading off to the right; follow it and cross the Sulby River on the footbridge. Follow the waymarkers along the eastern side of the valley where the river meanders its way along the valley bottom below. The path in part follows a recently built farm road. Be careful where it swings away at the mouth of the valley: the right of way goes down onto the Claddagh, through the ruins of Ballakerka Farm.

Follow the farm road onto the Claddagh and walk through the Claddagh until we join the right of way to Sulby Village, which we follow back to where we started, and from where we shall catch the first bus back to Douglas, either via Ramsey or back via Peel. If you are dependent on public transport, check the timetable in advance and plan the walk to suit, as the times vary winter and summer.

The Auldyn valley

**3½ hours
7 miles**

Nature has invaded the remains of quarry workings to make a fine goal for a walk from Ramsey.

TAKE the electric tram to Ramsey — we can still do this, summer or winter. Have you noticed how the staff and the local people who use the trams refer to them as electric cars. The only other place I have heard trams referred to in this way is in the United States and Canada. Many of the original American streetcars were built by G F Milnes & Co Ltd, of Birkenhead and maybe it is a real link with the past. Perhaps we have just travelled on the original rapid transit system.

There are no cafés or hotels on this walk, so we need to take some food with us.

From the tram station, we head off up Parsonage Road, passing the remarkable goods shed on the way up Mayhill onto the TT course, which we follow as far as the Hairpin Corner. We turn right and head off down the tree-lined roadway to Claughbane. Not so very long ago, this was all farmland and the extent of the housing development reflects the increase in the Island's population. On the left of the

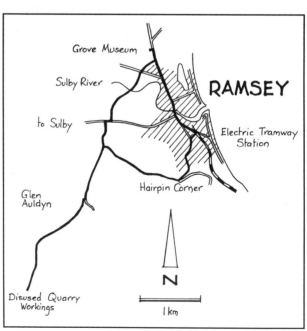

path is the Claughbane Plantation, soon giving way to an interesting range of hills.

As we pass through the uninhabited Crossags Farm, notice the rather insignificant stream we cross. Insignificant it may be, but it is worth more than a passing look. It is the Lickney Stream which passes under Parliament Square and the Town Hall on its way to discharge into the harbour. You can see it behind the filling station opposite the Town Hall when we are back in Ramsey. The old name for the stream is Strooan ny Craue, which means "the stream of the wild garlic" and it is the stream from which Ramsey takes its name, as the Norse "Ramsa" means wild garlic river. As we continue along the path we can see Ramsey Golf Course at Milntown on our right. The path has now become more rural, despite the proximity of the town.

Quite soon we join the Glen Auldyn Road, turn left and head up the valley under the flank of Sky Hill. At what looks like the head of the valley, be careful to cross the Auldyn River over the bridge opposite the old chapel, otherwise we shall end up at a dead end in Fern Glen.

The road carries on through the upper part of Glen Auldyn, passing some beautiful houses on the way. Just after the last house there is a turning place for vehicles, where we go through the gate ahead and continue along the now unsurfaced road, with the river on our left. The road is very muddy but with care we can pick our way through, passing the deserted shepherd's cottage, and swinging uphill to yet another gate.

Glen Auldyn in its full extent. The path to the quarry can be seen leading from the plantation.

Just through the gate, there is a delightful waterfall and then we leave all of the trees behind and Glen Auldyn (the swans' glen) opens up before us, with Clagh Ouyr and Snaefell at the head of the valley. The road, built on the side of the valley, used to give access to the slate quarries, now long disused. Nobody lives up here now but before 1900 it was a hive of activity with crofters and miners bringing prosperity to the area. Now we can only look at the remains of their life and guess what it was like to live and work in this now desolate valley.

Passing through a ruined farm with a few windswept trees framing the track, we cross a stream and come across a wheelcase just below the track, and what looks like an old magazine and office building. Then the road stops abruptly and we are at our hidden corner. Part of the quarry workings are now flooded and provide a wild, beautiful pond frequented by ravens and greybacks. Let's picnic and admire the view all around and down the valley.

You can see the marks on the rock face where quarrymen drilled the rock with hand jumpers ready for blasting. See on the right, as we look down the valley, where the rubbish was tipped in a spoil heap. It has been there for so long now that it looks like a natural part of the hillside, but from this angle we can see it for what it is.

The view down the valley varies dramatically with the seasons. The yellow of the gorse in spring, the dark green of the bracken in summer, and the sombre brown of the winter bracken which covers the valley from side to side. The valley was very foreboding, wet and gloomy, the day after Chernobyl blew up. I was there with my wife. We did not know about caesium at that time, but then it is difficult to avoid rain... and any fall-out it may have borne.

We have no alternative now but to walk back the way we came. The views down the valley do make it worthwhile. We continue as far as the main road, where we turn right for a short distance, passing the builders' merchant's yard, then left along Gardeners Lane, to the Whitebridge, crossing the Sulby River on the footbridge and going up to the Jurby Road, then right, then left along Richmond Road to the Andreas Road. Why this torturous route round the outskirts of Ramsey? To take in a visit to the excellent Grove Museum of Rural Life.

The return to town is by way of Bowring Road, which we follow into Ramsey. Just before we come to Jurby Road junction, look at the properties on the right and see if you can spot the remains of the Ramsey windmill, now converted into a house. As we pass Jurby Road, look out for St Olave's Church and look above the doorway at the ornate carving. We carry on down, to cross the Sulby River by Bowring Road bridge. The old name for Bowring Road was Bayr Geinee (sandy road), predating the bridge and still seen on the bilingual nameplates. We are soon in Parliament Street where we turn left at the Town Hall to follow Parliament Street all the way, past the Court House, to the tram station and our return to Douglas.

*An aerial view of the site of
Ballachurry fort on Walk Nº 8.
James Stanley, Earl of Derby
and Lord of Mann, saw the fort
as a means of defending the
Island against Cromwell and
the Commonwealth forces.
The fort is our hidden lunch-
stop.*

Repel the Roundheads

5½ or 3½ hours, 11 or 7½ miles

A walk into the old "lake district" of the northern plain which also recalls the bustle of Hall Caine's "airport". Allow 5 ¹/₂ hours for the full walk, or 3 ¹/₂ hours to Sandygate.

READ the bus timetable carefully before deciding whether to attempt the full walk or the shorter one. If the roads are closed for motorcycle racing, leave Ramsey by the Jurby Road and pick up the walk at Close Lake.

Take the tram to Ramsey and, from the tram station, cross the road into Peel Street and go along Parliament Street. Over the years I have developed an affection for this street and it remains at present the least disturbed of the town streets in all the Island. It perpetuates a fast disappearing way of life as far as shopping is concerned, offering, as it does, a great variety of shops, with ample opportunity to buy a snack for lunch as we walk through the street, to cross Parliament Square and go on into Lezayre Road.

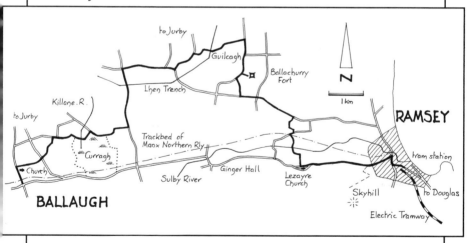

We soon reach the Ramsey Grammar Schools, with Sky Hill ahead of us. Quite a bit of this walk is on surfaced roads or even alongside busy highways, for which I apologise. But take heart, most of those flashing past in cars are not able to take in the views and admire some of the most beautiful trees on the Island, as we pass Ballakillingan, once the residence of EB Farrant, a director of the Manx Northern Railway and a promoter of the

Foxdale Railway. Quietly residing nearby is the former Manx Northern Railway locomotive, Thornhill, together with two carriages. Maybe someday we will see it in steam again.

Just ahead of us on the left, Lezayre Parish Church comes into view. It is one of those built on the instruction of Bishop Wilson and dates from 1835, but that is as close as we get to it. We turn sharp right opposite the church to go through Ballakillingan Farm (the name means farm of St Fingan's Church), following the footpath signs and stiles opposite the farm building and crossing the fields, eventually to join a farm street near the Sulby River. We cross the river by a footbridge, to continue along the track to the Garey (a name usually given to a stony or gorse-covered place).

We join the road just at the point at which the steam railway crossed it. There is no longer any obvious sign of its presence — even the lovely little stone-built station has gone — although careful scrutiny will just reveal the trackbed and the wide area where Lezayre Halt used to be. The gatehouse for the level

IMR Nº 11 Maitland, seen here crossing the Garey road and passing the quaint Lezayre halt, which had already fallen into disuse by the 1960s when this photo was taken.

crossing has been altered so much as to be almost unrecognisable. We shall see more of these gatehouses on other walks — those built by the Manx Northern were grand affairs, occupied by railway employees, well cared for and quite distinctive, with their hipped gables.

Turn right at the road and look for the signpost showing the way to the left leading across the fields. We walk a short distance down a farm road into a large field. The path skirts the head of the field to the left, alongside the hedge and then follows the long left hand boundary to a gate almost diagonally opposite us as we stand at the end of the farm road. Sometimes, if the field is in grass, we can cross it in a straight line. We then go through the gate and across a drainage ditch. This is part of the Lough Mallow trench which was built to drain the ancient Lough Mollo, referred to in the introduction. The purpose of draining these ancient lakes was to lower the water table and bring valuable land into cultivation.

From here the path goes straight across the next field to a stile in the hedge and out on to the Jurby Road. We turn left and head off for St Judes, taking care for traffic, as the road is twisty with no footway. We soon come to Close Lake Farm which is on the left of the road, opposite a small brick-built bungalow. The name again refers to Lough Mollo and we have just walked across part of its former bed. If we look into the field through the gate just before the bungalow, we can see a wooden pole with a finial on top, which is all that remains of Close Lake Airport. It is hard to believe that in the mid-1930s there were four flights a day linking the Island with Blackpool, with connections to Carlisle and Liverpool, three flights per week to Belfast, and the occasional connection to London. Passengers were taken to Douglas by a special bus service operated by Isle of Man Road Services, the company owned by the Isle of Man Railway Company. The hustle and bustle must have transformed this rural setting, with the sound of the three-engined Spartan Cruiser monoplanes. Several fruitless attempts have been made since the second world war to transfer the main airport from Ronaldsway to this site, to take advantage of the better weather and greater opportunities for expansion.

We must press on towards St Judes. We shall know when we are nearly there as the St Judes straight stretches ahead of us for almost a mile dead straight. Don't worry — we are not walking the full length of it, we are going to turn right half way down the straight, before we reach St Judes Church, and follow the narrow lane to Close-e-Cleator, where we join the Andreas Road, turning right towards Andreas.

Now we must be careful not to miss our hidden corner — no wonder Oliver Cromwell never came here! After about a quarter of a mile, we should see a sign directing us down the side of a field to an ancient monument. This is where we are heading and, after a quarter of a mile, here it is — a large earthwork, called Ballachurry Fort.

The fort was never completed beyond the earthworks. Built on the instruction of James Stanley, Earl of Derby and Lord of Mann, who was known as "Stanlagh Moar", it was one of a number of fortifications constructed to defend the Island against Cromwell and the Commonwealth forces. However, events overtook the Island. The Great Earl, with a force of Manx militia, supported the cause of Prince Charles, but was overrun at Wigan. He escaped but was eventually captured near Chester and executed. The Commonwealth forces laid siege to Castle Rushen and Lady Derby, without further bloodshed, became the last Royalist to be taken by the Commonwealth.

Walk round the wide top of the bastion and pause at each of the corners to look at the moat and ponder what it might have looked like had it been completed. We make our way back to the road and turn right towards Andreas, soon passing Kerroogarroo Chapel. As the road starts to climb one of the few hills in the area, we must look for the Guilcough farm entrance on our left, just before the crest of the hill, where we follow the right of way along the wide farm road and through the farmyard. On our way, we have a panoramic view of the major hills of the Island to the left and, unusually, a flat plain to our right. Unusual, because we have actually climbed up to reach this height, at which the land continues all the way to the sea, where it ends in the steep sand cliffs at Jurby.

The farm road now deteriorates and is much narrower as it drops down to a gate. Through the gate, curve left along the hedge to a concrete slab over a drainage ditch which we cross and continue into the field ahead. We follow the right hand hedge to the Lhen trench, which we cross by another concrete slab. It is worth stopping to look back along the trench towards the hills. You can see clearly the great gap of the Sulby Valley, cut by the Island's largest river, and you can clearly see how that river originally ran to the sea over this flood plain, first to the Killane and then through the area of the Lhen trench, before eventually meandering its way to Ramsey. The man-made trench follows the old course of the river and was first cut towards the end of the 18th century. It has been constantly improved and maintained since. As a result, the old lakes were drained, the water table lowered and all of this land brought into cultivation.

Over the bridge, we make our way to the right hand corner of the field to cross the hedge by the large tree, following the head of the field to join the Rhendhoo Road, then left again to join the Jurby Road where we turn right and follow the main road to

Sandygate crossroads.

If you have had enough, you can wait here for a bus back to Ramsey. On the other hand, if you are a glutton for punishment, come with me a little further and we shall try and find some of the remnants of the damp-sounding Lake Mirescog, now embraced by the Curraghs.

So, we go off to the left, towards Sulby on the A14 Sandygate Road, which soon starts to show signs of the boggy nature of the area, with abundant willows growing beside the road. The willow in the Manx is "yn shellagh" — we have always referred to them as "sallies" and, of course, the Latin name for them is Salix. The root of the name and how it came through to the Manx Gaelic is good for discussion which should happily occupy us until we reach the Old Sulby Road which forms a crossroads with the road we are on. We turn right and head off into the Curraghs.

The road was unsurfaced until recent years, but even so we can get the feel of what it was like because, even today, in winter, the water table in the surrounding land rises and we can see how easily this area could become waterlogged again, particularly if some of the drainage ditches like Anne Jane Wades or the Bishops Ditch were not properly maintained. Until the late 1960s, a drainage rate was levied on adjoining owners in the Sulby Drainage District and the Lhen and Kellane districts and these smaller ditches were part of this system. All are now maintained by central government.

We wander deeper into the Curraghs for about a mile and we come to a junction and, yes you've guessed it, we turn left, walking almost into the heart of the area. Follow the more defined track as it swings over a large drainage channel which is, in fact, the Killane River, some two and a half miles from where it discharges to the sea. Just look around as we walk. So much of the Island must have been like this in early times and, if nature had its way, it would in time revert to this. This is the last large expanse of the Island like it, although some sections remain in the Central Valley. Just as we came into the Curraghs quickly, so we leave the area behind, joining the Ballaterson Road and civilisation. Some 100 yards further on, take the left turn at the Dollagh Mooar. The place name gives the clue to the past. It means "the big black lake" — the Lough Dhoo referred to in the introduction. We continue to walk along the Ballaterson Road, crossing the much wider Ballacrye Road and heading for the tower of St Mary's, the parish church of Ballaugh. Turning left, we head for Ballaugh Village and the bus stop to take us back to Douglas.

As we pass the parish church, have a look inside. It is a typical Manx church, built in 1849. Look for the plaque on the wall commemorating Edward Forbes FRS, one of the Island's famous sons, giving a potted history of his life and achievements. When back at Douglas, look on the wall of the Public Library next to the Town Hall and you will find out where he was born.

(facing page)
IMR
N°4
Loch
starts
the day

Towering over Ramsey

2 hours
3½ miles

Our destination on this walk recalls a royal visit to Mann, nearly 150 years ago. This walk is not possible when the TT Course is closed for racing — check public notices during June and September.

IT is no mistake, many of our walks are unashamedly centred on the Manx Electric Railway, and here is another. This one has been coined especially with the 1993 MER Centenary celebrations in mind. Yes, it's off to Ramsey again, but let us try something different, particularly if we are walking in June or September (but remember the motor cycle racing).

For the centenary celebrations, a steam locomotive from the Isle of Man Railway was due to make a number of runs from Laxey to the Dhoon.

With a bit of careful planning, we might just be able to make our journey from Douglas to Ramsey incorporating one of the closed electric cars dating from 1893, as far as Laxey, then the steam train to the Dhoon and, finally, to Ramsey on a cross-bench open tramcar. Probably too much to ask for, but if we achieve it, then the trip will be unforgettable.

However we do it, remember to get off at Belle Vue Halt. We walk up the hill from the tram stop to the main road to Ramsey which we shall follow downhill for about a quarter of a mile, taking time to admire the view over Port e Vullen and Ramsey.

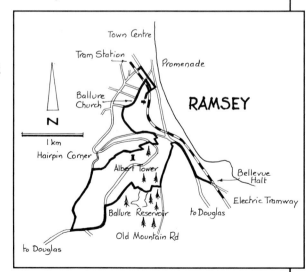

Just before we reach the entrance to Ballure Glen, look for a track on the left which appears to lead to a house. Look for the sign showing that it is an old public road unsuitable for motor vehicles. The sign shows a horse and a motor cycle and is peculiar to the Island, which has certain differences in the status of such roads compared with the rest of the British Isles. There are, for example, no bridleways, but this road was the old public highway to Douglas and, although no longer practical for motor vehicles, it still retains its status as a public highway.

So it is sharp left and up the rough stony road, through two gates and, about 150 yards past the second gate, look for the sign which directs us to the right, into the plantation. The track we follow takes an easy gradient through the Ballure Plantation then, suddenly, we go through a gate and there we are: Ballure Reservoir, our hidden corner, dominated by North Barrule, on the left. Some repair work has been carried out recently but hopefully we can walk across the head of the dam, built to serve Ramsey, and continue up the opposite side of the valley. A quick look down Ballure Glen as we leave the dam suggests the force of nature when the river cut its way to the sea.

We follow the track uphill, passing the disused Ballure farm, before joining the Snaefell Mountain Road. Take care — it is a busy road and we emerge on a corner. As soon as it is safe, cross the road and walk uphill, rounding the Gooseneck Corner, a famous vantage point on the TT Course. And what a setting — what other motorcycle race course can offer a backdrop like the one to our right over Ramsey and the northern plain.

Still climbing up the road on the northern flank of North Barrule, a few sparse trees appear ahead of us, on the left, by the ruins of Barrule Farm. Immediately opposite the farm, we look for the sign showing the public right of way leaving the road to our right. Follow the path alongside yet another of the streams that drain the vast boggy areas on North Barrule just above the 1,000ft contour. We lose height fairly quickly with views over Ramsey appearing now and then. We need to look for a gate on the right as we drop into the trees. We can not miss it — the sign on it states "To Tower" and that is where we are heading.

Head for the tree-lined stony crag and go through a second metal gate, following the main path and the right fork just a short distance after the gate. The path maintains the contour line below the crag and we keep bearing right. After the shelter, take a very sharp right turn, almost back the way we have come, zigzag uphill and there is the tower that we have seen elusively in the distance all through our walk. Not exactly a hidden corner, but nonetheless worth the effort to get to. Albert Tower, so called because it was built to commemorate the visit of Queen Victoria and Prince Albert in 1847, was erected on the spot where the prince stood to view the surrounding countryside. We can read the plaque above the door and also look at the numerous names carved in the stonework by people who have visited the monument. The names date back to at least 1859 — see if you can find an older one.

The view from the tower is splendid. The whole of Ramsey and the northern plain, Port-e-Vullen, and Maughold Head in the distance and, behind us, North Barrule. The North Barrule ridge is one of the more dramatic ridge walks in the Island now available to the public and worth the effort if you have the time.

Having savoured the view, it's back down the zigzag track to join the track we were on earlier, this time carrying straight on below the tower. We follow the path down the side of the hill which is unnamed but still part of the slopes of North Barrule, almost cliff-like where it joins the northern plain.

Be careful as we come close to the road, another path crosses ours left to right and we must go right, then down some rough stone steps to the road. Up to our right, we can see a signpost on the opposite side of the road and that is where we go.

Go through the gate and down the steps onto the path which leads down through Lhergy Frissell (Frissell's slope). John Frissell was a wealthy merchant and landowner, and Ramsey's first High Bailiff in 1777. Like so many of his contemporaries, he was a benefactor to the town and left a large tract of land for the enjoyment of its people. I wonder what John Frissell would think if he could see it now as we walk down to Ballure and see how the town of Ramsey has expanded to the foot of the mountain. Even Ballure Chapel is becoming surrounded on all sides, losing its rural setting.

On reaching the road, turn left until we reach the Crescent and turn downhill, following Crescent Road to Queens Drive, and right into Ramsey.

If you have time, go up Walpole Road when we reach the tramway, walking alongside the tram track. Pay particular attention to it and you will see that this short section is laid as street tramway, rather than railway — note too the ornate tram poles. At the top of the road, cross the tram track and walk up the right hand side for a short distance alongside the hedge, looking for a small gate leading to Ballure Church. There has been a religious building on this site since at least 1153AD and the present church was built at the instigation of Bishop Wilson in 1706, to replace an earlier chapel which, in turn, was built on the site of a keeill. The Frissell family vault can be seen in the graveyard. The church as now is, was restored in 1850. It seems a shame that this place, so steeped in history, is being surrounded with suburbia.

After looking at St Catherine's, Ballure, retrace your steps and follow the route of the tramway to Ramsey Station to return to Douglas.

Shortly after leaving Santon Station, the train heading south crosses the Santon Burn on the embankment referred to in Walk Nº 10.
(facing page) IMR locomotive head lamp

Not quite quoits

4 or 5¼ hours, 8½ or 11 miles

A fairly level stroll revealing some of the secrets of the southern plain. Allow four hours for the walk between Santon and Ballasalla and another 1¹/₄ hours if you carry on to Santon.

IF you were unable to enjoy the experience of travelling behind a steam locomotive on the electric railway, as described in the last walk, here's another chance to go for steam.

From Douglas, take the train to Santon — remember to tell the guard, as it is a request stop.

As we leave Douglas, the locomotive can be heard working hard climbing through the rock-lined cutting through the Nunnery. Suddenly we burst out of the dark cutting into the country, still climbing for almost a mile, passing Kewaigue and Ellenbrook, before climbing through the final rock cutting to Keristal, where we can enjoy superb views over the coast. The locomotive crew have a brief rest as they

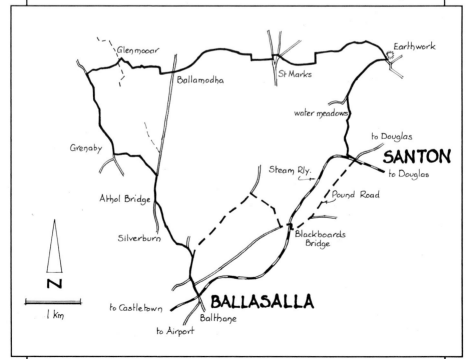

coast into Port Soderick station. After a run through the beautiful Crogga Glen, there is another climb to the highest point on the line at Ballaquiggin, and then a short run to Santon station. There is no platform here, so be careful as you step down. Santon is a typical Isle of Man Railway station, quite spartan in comparison with the grand buildings on the former Manx Northern line.

We walk through the gate beside the station building, turning right up the track to the main road. Cross the road with care and go over the stile by the railway bridge. The path follows the hedge at the top of the railway cutting, crossing two fields before going over a stile into the trees ahead of us. Walk down through the trees into the floor of the valley through which the Santon Burn runs, and follow the path across the fields to the river, pausing to look back at the substantial embankment which carries the railway across the valley (*see illustration on page 74*). The height and length of the embankment illustrates the fact that there is indeed a valley here — it diminishes rapidly upstream but, downstream, finishes dramatically in Santon Gorge. There is no doubt that this quiet river must once have been a raging torrent in the Island's formative years.

Follow the river for almost half a mile, crossing several stiles, until we come to a double stile over a fence and then over a hedge into a large flat tree-lined watermeadow at Mullenaragher, truly a hidden place. Be careful here to follow the footpath alongside the hedge and up the right hand flank of the valley. The map is useful here to avoid losing your way.

Once on the top of the bank, follow it, being careful when going through a wooden gate to carry straight on, swinging right and uphill to the next field gate. Avoid being deceived by the wooden stepping stile. Go straight on through the gate and follow the track across a rough piece of ground to join the surfaced road, which we follow uphill as far as the junction with an unsurfaced road leading to the rifle range. Turn left and follow this track, keeping the range on the right. Look out for the ancient monument just at the start of the track, which we shall stop and investigate.

If it is a clear day we shall be able to see South Barrule and the circular defence work on its summit. Did these earlier settlers have some form of structured society? I don't know anything about ley lines, but I often ponder on the fact that their dwellings often appear to be in straight lines. They are certainly in clear site of one another. This one is almost in line with Cronk ny Merrue, Ballakelly and the Braaid, which are all similar distances apart. The place to find out about these earthworks and the people who lived in them is the Manx Museum in Douglas. One thing I am sure about is that they must have been a hardy race judging from some of the places they lived, as we saw when we were on top of South Barrule. Let's carry on along the unsurfaced road towards Santon Burn, with South Barrule always ahead of us. As we drop down to the river, we can see St Mark's ahead of us. Cross the river and keep to the roadway, which is an ancient highway, and head uphill until we join yet another road by a gate. Go through the gate and turn left and here is another of the Island's little secrets.

Look at the large boulders lining the road. How did they get there? Was it the fairies? They must have been big fairies. Looking at them, it is clear they have come from Granite Mountain, at Foxdale. It is the same material that was used as secondary armour for the breakwater at Douglas. It is the most dense rock on the Island and hence the heaviest. I know how the stone got from Foxdale to Douglas but I can only guess how it came to be deposited all over St Mark's. Judging by the rounded appearance of the stone, it must have been rolled and washed down from the Foxdale area by meltwater at the end of the

Not quite quoits. The giant boulders at Ballakew.

Ice Age. As for the boulders beside the road, people must certainly have removed them from fields nearby to allow them to be culti-vated. We shall see more of these boulders in fields and hedgerows as we walk through St Mark's. Some of them weigh between two and three tons.

We follow the road past Ballakew to St Mark's, which comes into view as we top the hill. The chapel of ease at St Mark's is quite distinct and, framed between the hedges, looks almost Italian or Greek. The church was built together with the schoolhouse at the instigation of Bishop Hildesley to serve the parish of Malew.

We join civilisation at a crossroads. Look for the Millennium Way signs and cross over the road to follow the signs round the back of the old schoolhouse to the road leading to the Old Parsonage. Follow the waymarkers down the driveway, but be careful to go straight on through the kissing gate as the drive turns into the house.

We continue downhill for about 200 yards looking for a signpost showing a public right of way to the B30, off to the right. We follow it for a short way between the hedges to emerge into open rough meadow land. Turn sharp left and follow the hedge towards the road you can see in the distance. There are plenty of boulders lying around or built into the hedges and, at one time, there was a large standing stone, known as Godred Crovan's Stone. Alas, I can find no trace of it now. We cross the hedge into the road by an old stone stile and turn left.

This is the B30 or to give it its local name, the Bayr Ruy, and it leads to the Ballamodha (an anglicised corruption of the Manx, Balley Moddey, meaning "farm of the dogs").

The stream we cross at the bridge is the Awin Ruy (the red river) which drains from Granite Mountain and beyond, and is a tributary of the Silverburn. The granite on the mountain is slightly pink in colour, particularly when wet, and no doubt gave the river its name. There are several similarly named rivers on the Island, where the peaty soil contributes to the colour of the river, and this may be so in this case as well.

You may notice a little further on a small pets cemetery on our right, which is not such a well known place and certainly worth a passing look.

At the Ballamodha cross roads, pause before crossing the road and consider how straight it is. It was part of a 50-mile course used between 1904 and 1907 for the Gordon Bennett Cup motor car race. The Island saw the best cars in the world competing at speed for prestigious honours at a very early period of development of the motor car. I often think about the Island and its size and how it has always seen the latest technology of the day long before many people in large cities in Britain or Ireland. Think about the trains, the trams, cars, motorcycles and ships. It is still happening today with the BAe 146 jet, for which Manx Airlines was among the first customers, and the Sea Cat. This Atlantic Blue Riband holder, a vessel carrying cars and passengers capable of 42 knots, was launched in 1990 and visited the Isle of Man the same year. Many Island people sailed on it during its brief visit before it had made its trip up the Thames to the heart of London. It has now entered service elsewhere on the Irish Sea, but the vessel and its speed are a far cry from that of the first to ply routes from the Island to Britain, with its service speed of 8 knots.

Cross over the road, ignore the turning to the left and carry straight on through the gates to Cly Cur Farm. The map is essential here as we skirt the farmhouse, before coming to another set of gate pillars at the entrance to the farmyard. Look for and follow the hedge on the right, leading up to the stone-built house now used as a shooting lodge. At the house, cross through the gate into the large field which slopes down to a copse. Following the hedge, we soon reach the Awin ny Reash (river of the moorland), a major tributary of the Silverburn, draining the southern slopes of South Barrule. Cross the river and follow the track straight ahead, sticking close to the left hand hedge. Where the hedge kinks right, you should find a kissing gate stile which takes us into the adjacent field.

Consult the map and you will see that some field boundaries have changed. Walk through the gap in the hedge on the right and walk up the field to the gate at the top and then go through this and turn left, following the farm road. Look for the right of way signs that take us to Glen Mooar at the junction with the Beyr ny Skeddan (the Herring Way), which joins from the right, down the side of Glion Cam. With names like the "big glen" and the "winding glen", it is clear that these streams and river must have been bigger in earlier times. In fact, a number of dry river beds can be seen from the Corlea Road, providing further evidence of glacial retreat.

We are not going to follow the blue signs of the Beyr ny Skeddan. Instead, look for the waymarker on the gable of the barn at Glen Mooar and follow it into the field behind, and head off to Kerrowmoar, passing the farm buildings to join the Grenaby Road and turning left to follow it down to Grenaby.

At the bottom of the hill, look out for the stile on the left before the bridge. Climb the style into the meadow and follow the left bank of the Silverburn River (*see illustration on page 57*) where it has cut its way through the rock in a narrow gorge — yet another hidden corner, idyllic in summer and wildly aggressive in winter.

Follow the waymarkers and soon we shall find ourselves picking our way across the Awin ny Reash, again near to where it joins the Silverburn. We climb up the track, passing a ruined farm building and continuing along the old farm road until we join the Ballamodha Straight again at the top of Silverburn Hill. Turn right and walk down the hill to the Atholl Bridge where we join the path in Silverdale Glen to the left, following the Millennium Way markers to the boating pool and café where, if time permits, we can have a welcome break.

We leave the Millennium Way here and follow the hard-surfaced road instead, over the bridge past the old mill, walking straight on where it joins the Phildraw Road to Ballasalla. At the next junction, with the Crossag Road, we turn right and walk through Ballasalla quarter of a mile to the railway station where we can catch the train back to Douglas.

If you still feel like walking, there is an alternative finish to this walk. Instead of taking the right fork into Ballasalla when we join the Crossag Road, we can go left up Black Hill as far as the Orrisdale Road junction, which is the next road on the right. Follow the Orrisdale Road until it joins the main Douglas to Castletown road. We are turning left to the Blackboards Bridge but we have to cross the road. Take care — it is always busy and the traffic moves fast. The footway finishes before we get to the bridge, so it is single file, as the road is narrow. We shall cross over the bridge and turn right down the Old Castletown Road.

The railway runs under the road here and the bridge takes its name from wooden boarded screens which the railway company had to erect on either side of the bridge to deflect steam and smoke away from horses crossing, as there had been a number of incidents in which horses had bolted. The boards were painted black, hence the name. The black boards have long since gone, but the name has stuck.

We walk down the road, at the side of the valley of the Santon Burn, crossing the river by the bridge at Myllin y Quinney (Quinney's Mill). The mill is still there but is now a substantial private residence. As we pass it you will no doubt realise that we are now walking up the other side of the valley which many people pass but do not realise is there.

At the top of the hill as the road levels and swings right, look for the track leading off to the left. It is the Pound Road and it follows the eastern rim of the valley that I keep referring to. We shall walk along it to Santon Station.

You can see the main road crossing the bottom of the valley, having come down into it at Ballaglonney and climbing out of it at the Blackboards. The river meanders its way across a very wet area below us and the railway follows the western rim of the valley opposite as we walk along. As we approach Santon, we pass a water storage tank and, if we look to our left, there is the embankment carrying the railway across the valley and under the road bridge to Santon Station.

We join the main road and, some 100 yards along it, turn right to the station. If you caught the first train of the day to start this walk, you should be in time to catch the last train to Douglas, even if you stopped to eat at Silverdale.

If you have completed the whole circuit, you will have done well and seen some familiar places in, I hope, a different light.

An orchard but no apples

3 or 4½ hours, 5½ or 9 miles

Allow three hours to Ballabeg and another 1½ hours to Castletown. See also the variations (* page 85) to cater for the closure of roads for motorcycle racing.

THE second foray into the south uses the Steam Railway again to get to our starting point. We shall need to get off the train at Ronaldsway Halt. It is another request stop, so we must be sure to tell the guard. If you intend to do this walk in winter, when the steam trains do not run, take the No. 1 bus and get off at Ronaldsway Airport and walk down the industrial estate road

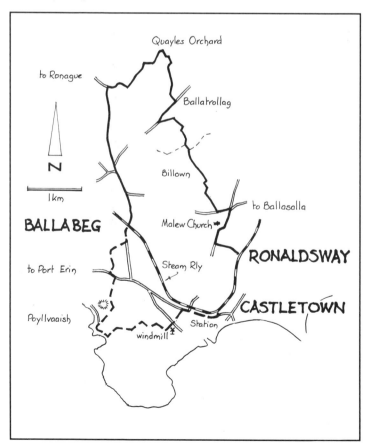

opposite the terminal building to reach Ronaldsway Halt.

After the train has gone, cross the track and head for the bridge over the Silverburn River as it runs its final course to the sea. After the bridge, the path goes straight ahead over Great Meadow, heading for the grey gate pediments of Billown House, which you can just see across the fields.

The path joins the main road opposite the entrance to Billown and we turn right along the road to the crossroads at Cross Four Ways, passing Malew Parish Church on the way. The church, repaired by that prolific church-builder, Bishop Wilson in 1747, is worth a stop and a brief look in the churchyard. There is a lot of history contained in the inscriptions on the tombstones. This was, after all, the parish church of the ancient capital of Mann, and the seat of Government. If the church is open, you will be able to read and learn more of the history of the Island and you will see that Illiam Dhone, who was shot at Hango Hill for alleged treason, was buried in the chancel.

At the crossroads, turn left and walk past the disused quarry, looking out for the right of way sign which will take us off to the right, up through the fields of Upper Billown. The ruin at the start of the path was part of the works associated with the quarry and a small plaque describes the method of working, which provided limestone for both building and agricultural purposes.

We walk along the edge of the quarry for a short distance and then go into the fields, following the hedge to our left, and the signposts, soon to join the farm road. We follow this to the right for about quarter of a mile where, on rounding a right hand corner, we find a gate ahead of us. Look for the sign showing that we go down left to cross a stream by a wooden planked bridge and then go into fields once again, through a kissing gate.

From here on the map is useful, as care is needed as we walk up the field alongside the ditch until we come to a stone stile, below Upper Billown Farm. Once across the stile, we continue uphill, still alongside the ditch, skirting the farm until we come to a ladder stile which takes us over the hedge into another farm road. We follow this straight on for a short distance until we come to a junction with yet another farm road. Here we must be very careful to turn left, heading towards South Barrule. Again, after a short distance, this farm street swings sharp left, but we go straight ahead into the fields through another kissing gate.

Once in the fields, the going is easier, as we follow the approximate line of the electricity supply poles across the field, to cross the boundary hedge between a pair of poles. We make for the top left hand corner of the next field, but we may have to skirt the edge of the field if it is in crop. Crossing a wooden

On the track from Ballatrollag. Quayle's Orchard is in the centre of the shot and South Barrule forms the horizon.

stile, we follow the hedge of the next field to cross yet another wooden stile and a short bridge across a ditch. If we follow the hedge on our right, this last field will bring us to the Ballamaddrell road. Before going through the gate, pause and admire the view over Langness, King William's College, and the distinctive keep of Castle Rushen. Port St Mary completes the panorama across the fertile southern plain.

Go through the gate and turn right. Walk along the road, passing Upper Ballavarkish, which is in the parish of Arbory. Ballatrollag is the next farm we come to. It is back in the parish of Malew, so we are almost walking the parish boundary.

At Ballatrollag, be careful because we have to turn left opposite the old farm to walk up the defined track alongside a modern bungalow. We follow the track between the hedges and it soon starts to drop downhill, towards a grove of trees, with South Barrule dominant ahead of us. It is a very pleasant view of the Island, not seen by many.

As we approach the trees, the track appears to continue through a river and on past the trees but, after going through the gate, we turn left before the river. Cross into the wood on the left and cross the Silverburn River by the footbridge. This is Quayle's Orchard — our hidden corner and lunch stop.

Have a look at the map while eating your lunch and trace the 200ft (60m) contour from Arbory, through Malew and Santon,

Lunch stop. The banks of the Silverburn river as it wends its way through Quayle's Orchard. Seen here in winter.

and you will notice that the major river valleys, although fed from higher ground, actually develop at this level. The tributaries and lesser streams generally ran from north to the south, as they drained the retreating ice sheet.

We follow the river through the glen to the stile at the end of the orchard. In winter this top end of the glen can be very muddy, but a path can usually be found to skirt the worst bits, and the footbridge which crosses back over the river can easily be seen.

Once over the river, follow the track past an old barn and cross the stile at the rear of Ballaglonney Farm into fields once again. Walking with the hedge on our left, we continue through three fields, before crossing a final stile onto a surfaced road. Follow this to the left and continue, noting the occasional right of way marker to reassure us, until we join the road from Ronague to Ballabeg. Turning left again, follow this road downhill to Ballabeg.

If you had to use the bus, then this is where you will have to wait for your bus back to Douglas. For those of us travelling by train, we have a little further to walk, going straight on at the bottom of the hill and crossing the road to the footway on the other side, to pass Friary Farm.

The name of the farm gives a hint about the past and relates to the period when the area was occupied by Bemaken Friary, in turn occupied by a Franciscan Order dating from 1373. As we walk past the entrace to the farmyard, you might just be able to make out the shape of the chapel which is all that is left of the friary, although the building is now incorporated into the barn surrounding the yard.

We walk on, keeping to the footway, straight on at Ballabeg three-roads to Lower Ballanorris — another classic Manx farm, with its imposing farmhouse and adjoining walled garden, now somehwat overgrown. A little further on we come to a bridge over the railway. We do not go over the bridge, but cross the road and walk down the tree-lined track, to the station at Ballabeg. Yes, it is a station and it even has a platform. It probably rates as the smallest in the British Isles and it is a request halt, so we must signal clearly to the driver that we want the train to stop.

* Now for the options and alternatives. Remember this is the Isle of Man and, on certain days in June and July, the roads which form the Southern 100 motorcycle race course are closed for racing. Racing motorcycles leap in the air over the bridge and the scene is considerably different from a normal tranquil day, so check the public notices in the newspapers or ask the railway staff, and if racing is taking place, then you must alter the start of the walk and get off the train at Ballasalla.

Starting from the station, turn right and walk through the village, straight on to Rushen Abbey. Take care at the second junction: you must go behind the Abbey Church to the river, which you cross on the footbridge, and follow the wall of the Abbey until you almost meet the main road again. There is a right of way sign on your right, directing you up the bank and into the fields, through Ballahot, to join another surfaced road after passing the farm. Where the farm street joins the highway, turn right and follow the road for a short distance before turning left up the Grenaby Road, and left again at Ballavell, to follow the wooden carved "Silverburn Experience" signs. After half a mile or so you join the original route and the complicated junction above Upper Billown with its ladder stile. But now you turn right to follow the route as described. When you reach Ballabeg, I'm afraid it has to be a return to Douglas by bus, but never mind, even this has its compensation as the route is very scenic and only used on these rare occasions.

Now I also mentioned an option. If you are keen and feel it is too early to wait for the train at Ballabeg, you can walk a little further for perhaps an hour and a half and return to Douglas from Castletown. I would certainly recommend this option in the height of summer when there are later trains running.

Instead of crossing the road to Ballabeg Station, stay on the footway and walk round the Iron Gate corner and along the

Ballakeigan Straight — names coined by the motorcycle fraternity and relating to the circuit. Half way along the straight, look for the track leading off to the right. Follow the old road to the top of Cross Welkin Hill and turn left where we join the main coast road. This section is described in Walk 12, but we only follow it as far as Poyllvaaish, where we turn left through the farmyard and cross the Awin Valloo (the Dumb River). At the second opening in the high stone wall, not more than 150 yards from the river, turn left and go into the fields to follow the river, which is really only a stream but so flat as to make not a sound as it meanders along the level area of Red Gap. The path is well signposted and follows field boundaries, zigzagging its way towards the distinct shape of the Castletown Windmill, which was built in 1828 but was, for many years, a ruin, with only the shape of the shell remaining as a substantial landmark. The path passes alongside the mill as it joins the road and we cannot help but marvel at the sheer size of the building. Imagine what it would be like with its cap and sails intact.

We cross the road and continue along the narrow path towards Westhill, passing the Buchan School, originally a private school for girls but now combined with the King William's College for boys. On the other side of the path is a new building, recently completed for a multi-national insurance company.

The original path is severed by a housing estate which we join and follow to the main road. The railway is in the cutting opposite, and we follow the line into Castletown and the station, to catch the train back to Douglas.

The petrified forest, cupolas and fairies

Walk
12

**4 hours
9 miles**

*A coastal walk with a taste, too, of mining antiquities.
Beware road closures in the racing season.*

NO, it is not a ghost story and no-one frightened the trees... This walk starts where the last one left off at Ballabeg Halt. To get there we take the steam train from Douglas to Ballabeg, remembering that it is a request halt. We also have to bear in mind the motorcycle racing in June and July when some of the public roads on our route are closed. Consult the local press to check on road closures and don't be deterred. If you have chosen a day for this walk that coincides with racing, just get off at Castletown.

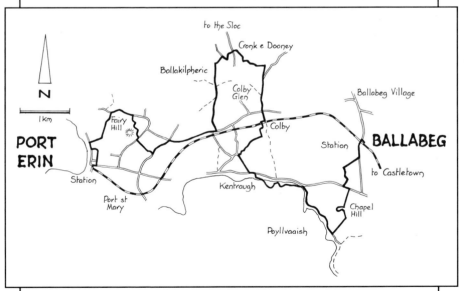

Walk into the town and, opposite the castle, follow the Coastal Path signs to Scarlett. Take the path as far as Poyllvaaish (Pool of Death), where you can join this walk. A full description of this section of Coastal Path appears in *The Isle of Man by Tram, Train and Foot*. At Scarlett, the Manx Nature Conservation Council has an interesting visitor centre beside the old quarry, with a short self-guided nature trail.

The petrified forest, cupolas and fairies

Walk
12

**4 hours
9 miles**

*A coastal walk with a taste, too, of mining antiquities.
Beware road closures in the racing season.*

NO, it is not a ghost story and no-one frightened the trees... This walk starts where the last one left off at Ballabeg Halt. To get there we take the steam train from Douglas to Ballabeg, remembering that it is a request halt. We also have to bear in mind the motorcycle racing in June and July when some of the public roads on our route are closed. Consult the local press to check on road closures and don't be deterred. If you have chosen a day for this walk that coincides with racing, just get off at Castletown.

Walk into the town and, opposite the castle, follow the Coastal Path signs to Scarlett. Take the path as far as Poyllvaaish (Pool of Death), where you can join this walk. A full description of this section of Coastal Path appears in *The Isle of Man by Tram, Train and Foot*. At Scarlett, the Manx Nature Conservation Council has an interesting visitor centre beside the old quarry, with a short self-guided nature trail.

87

From Ballabeg, however, we make our way up the track to the road, turn left and follow the road for a short way. We might just see the train in the distance at Colby as we cross the bridge over the railway. A short way up the Ballakeighan Straight, there is a right of way sign directing us to the right along the grassy lane described in the last walk. At the beginning of autumn, this lane abounds with blackberries and rosehips nearly as big as a child's fist.

Soon we emerge at the top of Fishers Hill or, more properly, Cross Welkin Hill, which is a corruption of the Manx name, now disappeared, but probably referring to a church on part of the Friary lands. We turn left down the road, then right at Balladoole Farm and follow the narrow surfaced road towards Poyllvaaish. But first, look for the sign on the right directing us to Chapel Hill, at Balladoole. It is a fortified Celtic iron age site and also a site of Viking occupation and ship burial. You can make a brief detour and have a look and, if you want to learn more about the history of the site, visit the Manx Museum in Douglas.

Back on the road, we pass the rear of Balladoole House, originally the home of John Stevenson, who, in 1704, was the Speaker of the House of Keys who was deputed to negotiate with James Stanley, tenth Earl. The negotiations led to the Act of Settlement, which redressed many grievances, the principal one giving Manx tenants security of tenure.

We soon arrive at the coast at Poyllvaaish — how would you like to live here in the middle of winter, particularly with a full gale blowing from the southwest? It must surely be the most exposed farm on the Island.

Turn right and follow the road along the coast. There is a superb view across Bay ny Carrickey (the bay of the rock), which takes its name from the Carrick Rock in the middle of the bay. Looking west across the bay, there is a superb view over Port St Mary, Cregneish and Mull Hill and you can see Milner's Tower, on Bradda Head above Port Erin. The area teems with bird life at all seasons. Even the choughs graze in the seaweed, often in threes, but more regularly in pairs, and many varieties of duck and geese can be seen, as well as the more common sea birds. See if we can find a Coayr ny Hastan (heron). If the tide is low, we may see one at the edge of the seaweed, waiting to strike, oblivious of the noisy curlews and oystercatchers.

I hope the tide is out because, as we come to the Shore Road, we can leave the road to drop down onto the beach across the sandy patch, heading towards the seaweed-covered area. Take care if you are not used to this sort of going as it is very slippery. We are looking for the fossilised roots and stumps of trees from a submerged forest. Local tradition has it that a freshwater spring within the beach assisted in the petrification of these remains.

Making our way across the rocks, we head back to the Shore Road at the sea wall in front of the three cottages. Following the top of the beach at the foot of the sea wall, look for the slipway leading up to the road, where we turn left and follow it as far as the Kentraugh East Lodge. Crossing the road, walk up the Kentraugh back road, following the estate boundary wall. Now and again, through the trees, we may catch a glimpse of Kentraugh Mansion, which is a beautiful house and the home of the Gawne family. When we passed Balladoole earlier, I referred to the House of Keys whose members, prior to 1867, were self-elected. The last Speaker of the

The ornate rear entrance to Kentraugh Mansion

non-elected Keys was EM Gawne, of Kentraugh, who had held office since 1854. The size of the estate can be gauged as we walk past the rear of the house and the cupola above the ruined barn, which was gutted by fire more than 50 years ago, but whose walls remain. Observe the profound axiom above the ornate doorway:

Judge not your fellow man's condition,
Until you be in his position.

A little further along the road, we must look for a right of way through a gate on the right, just after we cross the Colby River. We walk straight across the field to the gorse and, with a little care, find a pathway through it to cross a footbridge over the river. Now we can see the fertile southern plain where land was much sought after in early times. Aim for the gateway straight across the next field — note the classical Manx round gate pillar, with its conical coping and the stone stile adjoining. Once over that we cross the next field, heading for the ruins of Ballacreggan (farm of the craggy land). On reaching the hedge, it is sharp left, following the hedge back to the river which we cross again by another bridge. Immediately the other side, the path follows the river upstream to Colby Village. We have to cross the railway line and care must be taken. If we are lucky, we might just see a train crossing the delightful shallow stone-arched bridge which spans the Colby River.

Follow the path to the main road which we cross, then go right over the river once again, turning left past the ornate clock, up the Colby Glen Road, walking through the old part of Colby which has not lost too much of its old charm and character.

As we leave Colby, we start to climb a little and we must look out for the entrance to Colby Glen, yet another of the Island's National Glens. Go through the gate, down the bank and, yes, cross the river yet again, then follow it upstream. The habitat is perfect for the grey wagtail and it can often be seen, flashing yellow as it flits from stone to stone, dodging the water. The river, though small, cuts through a rocky gorge and can be very spectacular in winter. The path climbs over this part of the glen to open out into a natural amphitheatre of trees. Our path is off to the left, up the stone steps, but first, just walk on a little to the seat ahead and take in the tranquillity of this beauty spot with the pond and the trees with their nesting boxes all around us. A good place for a break.

Now we go back up the stone steps and pass a rock outcrop. It is worth stopping to climb onto this and look at the river below, as it drains the land from the slopes of Cronk ny Irrey Laa. We continue up to a kissing gate stile and then go right on a farm road between hedges, to Cronk-e-Dooney (Church on the Hill). The view to the left overlooks the trees of Kentraugh and, to the right of Kentraugh, is Port St Mary.

Be careful where we join another right of way at a T-junction — we turn left and are now on another farm road, which we follow, being careful to turn left at the farm, passing a good example of a stone barn, before reaching Ballakilpheric Methodist Chapel, dating from 1850. Cross the road and skirt round the chapel, following the public right of way sign. We are on a surfaced road and soon go through Ballakilpheric (the farm of Patrick's Church) and past the entrance to a beautiful house called Burnbrae. Ahead of us are the Carnanes and Ballarock, but we must be very careful here not to miss the latch gate and the sign to Scholaby.

Yes, we are going to walk through the garden of the house, which you have no doubt been admiring. Take care and remember you are on private property and respect it. We follow the fence to an ornamental pond and, looking for the waymarkers, cross the drive and follow the path across the front of the house, passing the duck pond, before reaching the ruined building and a stile which takes us into the fields again. A hidden corner? Well, yes — I suppose it is. I well remember walking this path when it was very different, back in the early 1960s. In those days it was no more than a little ruined farmstead.

So, ahead of us, is Scholaby Farm and that is where we are going, across two fields and through the farmyard, which is always muddy, and then down the farm road to the main road to Port Erin. On the way down, look at the chimney and ruins on the right. There are more just below Ballacorkish Farm. These are the surface remains of the Ballacorkish Mine, one of the more successful enterprises, which produced lead ore and zinc blende. There were three shafts — King, Phosphate and South. The workings reached a depth of 75 fathoms (138 metres) and work ceased about 1895.

At the main road, turn right and walk along the pavement as far as Ballakillowey crossroads, then left and continue as far as Rushen Parish Church. If you go to look at the church, which dates from 1775, cast your eye over the gravestones on the left of the path through the churchyard and be amazed at the young age at which many people died. Life must have been very hard in those days.

Back to the lychgate, pass the old vicarage, and go along the Barracks Road to join the main road again. Now we must take care. Cross the road and turn right towards Ballafesson and cross a stream, ignoring the stone stile in the wall. Next there is a gate and we go through it, following the hedge line to a second gate. Consult the map — it is easy to lose our way here. Go through the gate and we are in a field with a huge mound on our left. The Norse people did indeed call it Howe Mooar (the big mound). It has, in more modern times, been called the Fairy Hill and the nearby housing estate reflects that in the name of the estate and its street names. Was this mound of earth built by the Vikings, later to be used as a defensive fort by others? You should make a point of visiting Castle Rushen where there is a full description of it.

From the gate, cross to the hedge immediately opposite and follow it round to yet another gate, a little more difficult to cross as there is a small ditch here as well. Then we follow the hedge to the road, turning left to Honna Hill and Bradda East. As we start to climb the hill, look for the stile in the wall on the left, opposite the old chapel. We go through it onto Rowany Golf Course and, looking out for flying golf balls, walk into Port Erin, making sure we go over the gorse-covered mound in the middle, and sticking to the right of way, which is clearly marked.

Joining the road by the clubhouse, let's go right onto the promenade and take the scenic route into the village, following the promenade round into Station Road. If we have time before catching the train back to Douglas, the Railway Museum is worth a visit, particularly in 1993, the Year of the Railways.

The lady and the thieves

5½ or 8½
hours, 11
or 17 miles

Allow 5½ hours for the walk as far as Sulby and another 3 hours if you go on to Kirk Michael. This walk is not really practical during TT race week.

LEAVE Douglas on an early tram to Laxey and take refreshments for this full day's walk. From Laxey Station, walk to the main road and head for the Laxey Wheel along Mines Road, passing

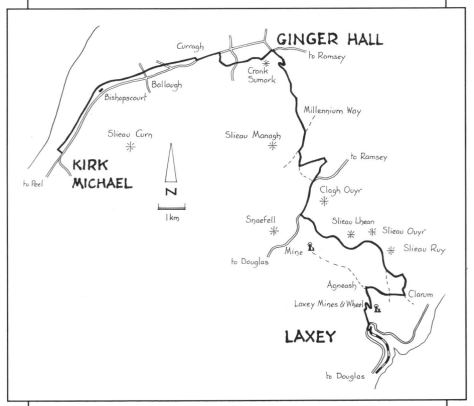

former miners' cottages.

We start to climb towards Agneash, beneath the wheel which towers ahead of us, and then turn left and continue uphill until we reach the village green. The wheel and the mine workings are all fully described in *The Isle of Man by Tram, Train and Foot*, but I can not resist telling you again that the diameter of this, the world's largest water wheel, is 72ft 6ins. It was built to pump water from the mine workings, and it did this by means of a series of pumps, lifting water into sumps at different levels until it reached the adit level, from where the water drained by gravity to the Laxey River. On the way up Mines Road, almost opposite the fire station, you might have noticed some work being carried out on the opposite side of the valley. This is where it is hoped eventually to develop a true "underground experience" opening up the adit to access the gallery in which the Man engine is located. This was a hydraulic engine with a 12ft stroke, providing a means of lifting men to the surface from every gallery from a depth of 200 fathoms (370 metres).

The adit was serviced by a 19-inch gauge railway and two engines, the "Bee" and the "Ant" had access underground to all of the shafts.

At Agneash, look for the right of way sign and the track which falls steeply away from the village and crosses the river on a wooden bridge parallel to the old stone one which has collapsed. Take care, the wooden steps are often very slippery with moss. Once up the steps, go right through a kissing gate and follow the track through the gorse to the surface remains of Dumbells shaft. As we cross Glen Drink, look left and you will see the remains of four stone arches which carried an aqueduct and water from the tail race of the water wheel which was housed in the large building ahead of us. This water was used again to power another wheel at Agneash.

We climb past the remains of the Dumbell machine house, which originally housed a substantial water wheel. Judging by the size of the wheelcase, it must have been almost 50ft in diameter. The wheel was replaced by a turbine in the 1870s and a steam engine was also fitted in the building. All of this equipment was used for winding and it served Dumbells Shaft, which at 302 fathoms (558 metres) below adit level, was the deepest of the Laxey shafts. The adit here is about 54 fathoms below us, so the bottom of Dumbells Shaft and the deepest workings of the mine are 356 fathoms below where we stand: that is 2,136 feet (329 metres). It would certainly not have done to suffer from claustrophobia and it is no wonder that the man-engine was installed to lift the miners to and from the workings. It was a long way to climb down and it must have seemed even harder coming back at the end of a day's work.

We go out through a gate into the field behind the machine house and climb diagonally to the top right hand corner. The stone structure in the field is the cistern which provided the head of water for the later turbine, the penstock to the machine house being buried in the field. As we climb over the stile at the top of the field, look back over the village of Agneash and across the valley where the Snaefell Mountain Railway track can be clearly seen, perched on the side of Cronk y Vaare.

Turn right and follow the right of way past Glen Drink and over the stone wall at Croit ny Cloughbane, along a short section of rough road to its junction with another road coming up from Laxey. Turn right and then left after a short distance to follow the right of way across the fields to the Clarum. We join the Clarum Road, which is surfaced, and turn left to the mountain gate, which we cross onto the mountain land. If you have not used the map so far to help you, I would say it is essential now... There is an old mountain road here which is difficult to pick out. We have to be careful and try to follow the route on the map over the Dreeym (ridge) under the southern slopes of Slieau Roy (the red mountain). Don't be tempted to take the short cut straight across — you will end up in a bog up to your knees.

Soon we start to pick up the shape of the old road as we head north and we can see it plainly, skirting round below the saddle between Slieau Ouyr (the brown mountain) and Slieau Lhean (the broad mountain) and that is the way we are going — a good steady uphill walk!

The road is cut by a gully which we have to clamber down but there is a little hidden corner here, with a pool feeding through a hole in the wall. Look through it and there, framed like a picture, is the pointed summit of Beinn y Phott (pronounced, corruptly, "penny pot"). Carry on uphill and, just as we leave the mountain wall, look out for a stone-lined conduit, deflecting water off the mountain, down to Glion Ruy and Glion Agneash, to supplement the water supply to Ballacregga Reservoir, which we can see below us. Yes, it was built by the miners, who sought to catch every bit of water from the surrounding hills to provide power for their winding wheels and for the pumps to keep the mines relatively free from water. Once the pumps stopped working, the mines flooded to the natural level of the adit. It does not do to think too much about this, as it seems rather like banging your head against a brick wall.

Soon we reach the saddle between the two hills — Gob ny daa slieau (the point of the two hills). Another miners' path used to cross here, linking Agneash to the North Laxey Mine in the next valley. Unfortunately, its existence as a public path was not proven in 1973, when the Rights of Way Act, 1961, came into force, and the lower part is lost. Just think about the conditions you would have faced working in North Laxey Mine, about 600ft below ground. You would have been working in running water with a pick, hand-balling stone out of a narrow drift in the hope that some of it contained valuable ore. The only light would have from a candle stuck in a lump of clay on your hat. The drift often reduced to the thickness of a thread but you had to continue following it in the hope that you would find the "mother lode".

Then, at the end of your day, you would have to climb (no man-engine here) back up the 600ft by almost vertical ladders. At least then you only had three miles or so to walk home, but you had to climb 750ft from the mine to the saddle here, before going down into Laxey. If it was raining, it did not matter because you were wet through anyway. But imagine what it was like in the middle of winter, blowing a gale from the south-east and hail! It was a brave man who went home in that. They were heroes. I sometimes think that I can see those men, you know.

But back to walking: carry on round the flank of Slieau Lhean and follow the road to the Black Hut on the Snaefell Mountain Road. Do you know, I have just realised that the black hut has gone. It was a tarred galvanised shed used by the Highway Board for years as a store and shelter for workmen. It was still there a couple of years ago — but at least the name survives. Watch the bog on the way down, it pays to cross the wall for a short distance to avoid the worst part.

Once at the Mountain Road, turn right and follow the road for half a mile to the next mountain shelter, at the Mountain Box. We have to watch out for the traffic as there is no footpath and they take no prisoners! Perhaps we should walk on the mountain land alongside the road — it could be safer. When we get to the shelter, there are two gates. Look for the one overlooking Ramsey and you will find the words "North Park" cut into the gate. This is our route.

Roger Marshall and Steve Hislop duelling during the 1988 TT in this photo taken from the Mountain Box, Snaefell

There is no right of way marked on the map but this was originally Crown land and is now owned by the Manx Department of Agriculture, Forestry and Fisheries. There is a right of ramblage over the land, but remember it is tenanted for grazing so we should, as always on the mountain land, respect the country code. If you have a compass or if the visibility is restricted, head off on a bearing of 42°. Otherwise, we can keep Ramsey in our sights and we shall soon start to walk downhill and it will become apparent that we are on the left hand side of a river. This is

Glion ny Maarliagh (glen of thieves), a fairly common place name on some of these river gorges, particularly if they are deep and twisty. Let us stop and look at the head of the glen with its very unusual formation of mounds. The watercourse which starts on the side of Clagh Ouyr is the Auldyn River which we follow along its left bank, aiming towards the mountain wall above Glen Auldyn, and our bearing should bring us out on the point of the wall where we can stop for a picnic. Perched on the steep bank below the wall, we overlook a hidden corner with a pretty waterfall dropping into the gorge below our feet.

Waterfall at Glion ny Maarliagh

Suitably refreshed it is off up the steep hill behind us, alongside the mountain wall. I did say steep! We soon come to a right-angle bend and there appears to be an old stile in the wall straight ahead: ignore it — we turn left and continue upwards, following the wall to the top of the hill. Where it levels out, we come to a point in the wall where three boundaries meet. We have to climb over the wall. Once over, there is a track just a few yards away and we follow it to the right across the open mountain, through the bog, which is always difficult. We soon rejoin the wall, which we cross through a metal stile, following the well-defined track which, at this point, is part of the Millennium Way. We have to keep a look out for the public right of way sign pointing to Narradale (grid reference MR 408915). It is certainly a junction in the middle of nowhere. When we find it, turn left and head off over the open moorland quite near to areas covered in earlier walks, but presenting us with different views. You can see Slieau Managh on our left and now that you know where to look, can you see Creg Bedyn? This is one of those tracks which can be glorious in summer hell in winter, as there is absolutely no shelter at all.

Soon we come to the mountain gate and the road becomes more defined, between hedges, and then, as it steepens, it is surfaced. All the time there is a commanding view over the northern flood plain of the Sulby River. There is a good view of Cronk Sumark from this road, just as we turn a corner into the tree-lined glen above Ballamanagh. Cronk Sumark is a distinct small hill commanding a strategic position and it is no wonder that it became the location for a hill fort for successive occupants. The Norse name for the hill meant "short ridge", although its present name means "primrose hill". It's certainly a good place to roll hard-boiled eggs at Easter.

We continue downhill to the Ginger Hall Hotel, where we join the main Ramsey to Kirk Michael Road and if you have had enough, we can stop here and wait for a bus to Ramsey and then return to Douglas by bus or tram.

If you want to do a bit more rail trail-walking, we can carry on to Kirk Michael, in which case we go left along the Claddagh Road below Cronk Sumark. Remember we have been near here on Walk No.6 but we have an opportunity on this walk to go up to the top of the hill, following the route signposted by the Manx Museum. It doesn't take long and is worth the effort, and you will see why it became a hill fort site.

Back down again, and we cross the Claddagh (river bank) to Old Sulby Village, crossing the Glen Road and walking straight on along the Old Sulby Road until it joins the main road again. Here we turn left, cross the road and walk along the footway, passing Gob e Volley quarry. It is now disused, but has given its name to a stretch of the TT course — Quarry Bends. The road was widened here in 1986 to meet the demands of modern traffic and is considerably changed. Can you imagine riding a racing motorcycle through here at speeds approaching 150 mph. It happens every year in June and September. When we reach the entrance to the Curragh Wildlife Park, leave the road and walk towards the entrance. Turn left before the entrance and walk along the disused railway track bed. You can even see some remnants of rail here if you look carefully. We follow the railway through to Kirk Michael. It is a pleasant walk and you might just be able to see why Ballaugh parish is so called. It should be spelt Bal ny Laghey, meaning "place of the lakes or bogs".

The approach to Kirk Michael past Bishopscourt is perhaps the most interesting part of the walk. Imagine the train curving out of the Bollyn Road cutting onto the embankment, and sweeping past Bishopscourt. It is very hard to grasp that in the early 1950s, I got on and off the train at Bishopscourt, which was a request halt, while I was surveying the buildings. I was an articled pupil to Wilfred Quayle, the Diocesan Surveyor. On one occasion, Jack Lowney, driving No.5, Mona, came round the curve into view.

We were expecting him to stop but he had forgotten about us and we had to leg it after the train carrying staffs and theodolites. He managed to stop some distance up the line. They were interesting days then and the pace of life was different. One thing about walking and I have said it many times, you certainly have time to think, reminisce and philosophise — maybe even put the world to rights.

After the deep cutting at Orrisdale, the line took a straight run into Kirk Michael through what was then all fields, running behind the parish church to arrive at the station. The buildings survive but, as you can see, are now used as the local retained fire station. At Kirk Michael it is up Station Road into the village to wait for the bus back to Douglas.

This last option is for the really energetic walker who is after a good long day out, but I have not forgotten the less energetic. How about this for an easy summer option? Take the Snaefell Mountain Railway from Laxey to the Summit of Snaefell, taking in the views all round, then walk down the mountain to the Black Hut and join the walk there as far as the Ginger Hall Hotel. That should take you three hours, during which you will see all the best bits, and can be done whilst the roads are closed for motorcycle racing. You may have to wait for the roads to open at the Ginger Hall, but the company will be convivial.

14

Hiding your light under a bushel

**Full day
7 miles**

A boat trip from Port St Mary to the tranquillity of the Calf of Man — and a few things to see when you get there.

THIS walk is a little bit different, and it can only be done in the summer season. We are going to the Calf of Man and the trip takes a full day. Make sure it is sunny and not too windy — there is nothing worse than a cold miserable day on the Calf, and in any event, if the sea is too rough, the pleasure boats do not sail.

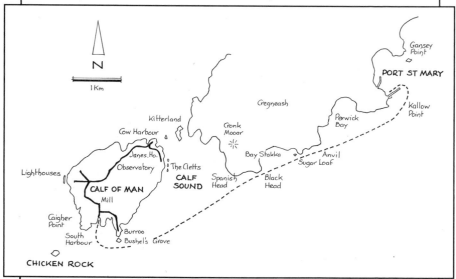

The Calf of Man lies south of the main island and is clearly visible from the coastal footpath. It is separated by a strip of water known as the Calf Sound, which can be navigated by small vessels, although it is noted for its treacherous currents and other hazards to navigation, of which the principal ones are the Thousla Rock, which is submerged at certain states of the tide, and Kitterland, a small island of just under a third of an acre.

Calf Island is uninhabited, except for lighthouse keepers and a warden who lives at the Bird Sanctuary and records the passage of migrating birds. The old farmhouse, which is used by the warden, is run by Manx National Heritage, (formerly the Manx National Trust) and, on application, limited bunk accommodation is provided.

The Calf extends to about 1,000 acres and has one road which links the two principal landing places, Cow Harbour and South Harbour. There is a loop off this road which gives access to the lighthouse. Once on the island, you can have about three to four hours to ramble at will and all I intend to do is point out some of the places worth visiting.

Pleasure craft run trips to the Calf from Port Erin and Port St Mary at roughly hourly intervals and subject to demand. The trip from Port Erin is shorter and lands at Cow Harbour and the one from Port St Mary, depending on the weather, usually lands at South Harbour. I prefer the Port St Mary trip for the more rugged cliff scenery that we pass on the way to the Calf.

So here we go. We leave Douglas by the steam train and head south, to alight at Port St Mary. Be sure it is the first train of the day as we need as much time as possible. From the station, we walk down Station Road into the village. Buy some picnic provisions if you have not already thought that far ahead. Continue down the High Street to the harbour and head for the breakwater, looking for the sign by the steps advertising trips to the Calf. Check the return timings. We have to sacrifice the return train journey at certain times of the year and use the bus.

It takes about half to three quarters of an hour to reach the Calf. On leaving Port St Mary, we pass Kallow Point where the shelving rocks can give rise to some nasty waves in rough weather. Once past this point, the boatman will usually sail close in to the cliffs at Koine-e-Ghoggan (headland of the chasms). You will see fulmars nesting on the peculiar ledge formation of the rock here. As we follow the cliff we may see common seals — we will certainly see cormorants and shags in abundance.

The cliffs continue to rise more steeply above us, before opening up to reveal a small bay in the centre of which is a large rock, known as the Anvil, or Pulpit. There is a cave behind it and also another to the left of it as we look from the boat. This cave penetrates the headland to emerge behind Sugar Loaf Rock, a nesting place for fulmar, kittiwake and guillemot, its splendid isolation providing a magnificent and secure home for their young. The name of the bay is Norse in origin, Baie Stacka, and means "bay of the rock". You will see that the rock face behind the Sugar Loaf is shattered and riddled with deep clefts. It is aptly named the Chasms.

Next we round Black Head and it too has a dramatic cave on its southern face. The land slopes steeply into Slea ny Bery and, on the left of the bay as we look at it, is the sheer, almost vertical, sheltered north face of Spanish Head, towering 300ft above us.

Then, suddenly, we leave the Island behind and find ourselves looking through the Sound. There is Kitterland, and you can also see the Little Sound. We approach the Calf at Kione Roauyr and you can see some rocks nearby which are submerged at certain states of the tide. These are the Cletts (rocks) and are freqented by seals. At low water you will see them lying on the rocks and will almost certainly hear their eerie, almost human, cries. Kione Roauyr (broad headland) is almost 250ft high and you can see the land sloping down almost to the sea ahead of us. It ends in a promontory with a hole through it, the Burroo, meaning, appropriately, "the eye". We pass the next headland, Kione ny Halby (Scottish headland) and suddenly there is South Harbour and our landfall.

Jump ashore and the boatman will tell you when to be there for collection. Now your time is your own to do as you please for the next couple of hours. Just lie in the sun, watch the rabbits and wallow in the tranquility. If you want to come with me, then let's first walk down to the Burroo and look for "Bushel's Grave". Who was Bushel? you may well ask. He is not, as far as I understand, buried here and it is not clear whose the remnants are. One thing I do know is that the view north is superb and, to the south, we can look across the bay known as the Puddle, towards Caigher Point, and see clearly the lighthouse which was built on the Chicken Rock in 1875. It was severely damaged by fire in 1960, since when it has been reduced to an unmanned light and fitted with a flashing beacon and an audible warning system. The rock on which it stands was a hazard to shipping and we shall soon see the original lighthouses built to warn vessels.

Making our way back to the boathouse, now used as a store and garage by the Commissioners of Northern Lights, we make our way up the pathway which skirts the old field boundaries of the farm which was last worked in 1939. We cross the head of Rarick and start to walk inland uphill towards the ruins of what used to be the farm watermill. This is where we try to follow the track out to the left towards the lighthouses which have now come into view. Sometimes the growth of bracken, which can be chest high, makes the path difficult to follow and caution should be exercised when the bracken is in spore. The path eventually joins a more distinct one leading past some old ruined farm buildings, built low behind the wall to provide shelter for the animals. Now ahead of us is the new lighthouse with its powerful light, visible for 20 miles.

I clearly remember it being built and made several trips to the Calf to watch the work in progress. All of the building material was shipped to Port St Mary breakwater and stored in a compound from which it was carried by helicopter to the building site. The work was completed in 1967 and the light came into service straight away, replacing the lighthouse on the Chicken Rock. This, in turn, had replaced the two older lighthouses on the hill behind us, which had been built in 1818. I think they are worth a closer look to admire the construction and perhaps wonder how they got their materials to the site. One thing is certain, they did not use helicopters!

If we can make it, we could perhaps reach the highest point on the Calf, above Amulty, where the summit is a little over 420ft above sea level. This is where Bushel, the hermit, is supposed to have lived. Now I can apologise for the title of this walk.

Calf of Man lighthouse being built in 1968

Let's retrace our steps to the road and head for the farm building and see what activity there is. We may see birds trapped in the nets for ringing and recording their size, weight and so on, or for logging if they are already ringed. The farm buildings were last used for their original purpose between 1935 and 1939 by Mr R E Garrett, who ran sheep and cattle and worked the land with four horses. The farmhouse is supposed to be haunted by a one-legged sailor who can reputedly be heard walking about on his wooden stump.

Continuing through the gap between the two hills, the road emerges onto the north side of the island, to command a superb view of the Isle of Man and its west coast, up to Bradda Head. On the way down, look for a track to the right (it might be overgrown), leading to a house, the roof of which we might just be able to see. This is "Jane's House", so-called, from where the view north is beautiful — fancy living here. Well, it may not be so idyllic in the middle of winter with a full north-west gale blowing.

Return to the road and go down as far as it goes, to Cow Harbour, so called because it is here that the cattle were landed after swimming over from the mainland, cajoled by the owner alongside in his boat. Seems a bit risky to me, but they did it. The slipway is modern, of course, and this is the landing place for the boats from Port Erin. Let us just walk around the corner towards Fold Point and you will see the old Grant's Harbour. This, for me, is the ideal setting for a romantic period film — link it to the old lighthouses and the house and it would make Wuthering Heights seem like downtown London!

Go on a bit further to the Cletts and, if you don't make a noise or move too quickly, you will almost certainly get a good view of the seals that frequent this area. Having taken all of that in, we should just have nice time to walk back across the Calf to South Harbour to wait for our boat to take us back to Port St Mary to catch the train or bus back to Douglas after a peaceful, relaxing day away from it all.

An island surrounded by land?

3 ½ hours
7 miles

A taste of the southern hills and, arguably, one of the finest coastlines in the British Isles.

WE have to take the train or bus south to Colby to begin our quest for an island surrounded by land. From the station, we walk up Station Road to Colby Bridge and turn right, heading for Ballabeg and, after about half a mile, we shall come to Cronk y Thatcher housing estate. If you caught the bus this is, in fact, where you should get off.

Just past the estate entrance, look for the right of way between the houses, to the left. That is our route — straight up into the fields to follow the stiles and signposts to Ballagarmin. The right of way passes the gable of Ballagarmin and the stone stile is right up against the house. Once in the field, you can trace the line of the old farm road curving up through the middle of it, to the ruined house on the skyline which is where we are heading. Go through the gated stile into the muddy lane and turn right. Follow the lane, which is lined with gorse and brambles, for a short distance. It opens out to confront us with gates everywhere, but the lane goes straight across the open area, now tree-lined and quite wide. It is quite lovely and a hidden place in its own right. The map will help, but

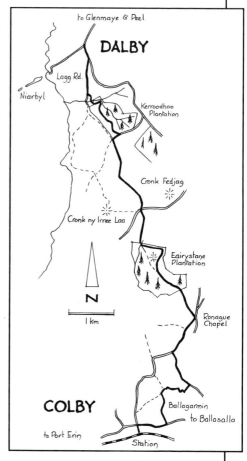

the lane is quite easy to follow and, after a while, we join the Ballagawne Road by the last of a number of stone stiles built into the side of the stone gate pillars.

Turn left and continue up the surfaced road to join the Colby Glen Road above the covered reservoir at Earystane. Turn right and follow the Colby Glen Road as far as Ronague Chapel (now a private residence) and look for a rough track on the left, just past the chapel, which leads to Earystane Plantation on Slieau Earystane, the hill above us on our left. Just as we enter the plantation, pause and look back at the view of the southern plain, with Langness peninsula and lighthouse in the background, and Castletown and its castle in the centre of the panorama. Enter the plantation through the gate and follow the wide grassy track between the trees. We climb steadily almost to the top of Cronk Lhost (the burnt hill). Straight ahead of us, framed by the trees, is the summit of Cronk ny Irrey Laa. Ignore the left fork and keep to the main track to the top of the hill where a view of the Sloc (the hollow or pit) opens below us, framed between Lhiattee ny Biennee and Burroo Mooar.

Be careful here and look for the narrower track off to the right and follow it through the smaller windswept trees over the crest of Cronk Lhost. The track appears to come to a dead-end by the boundary wall, so turn left and follow it along the eastern side of the hill, overlooking what I would say is the finest view of South Barrule, which makes the detour worthwhile. Carry on along the stone and sod hedge until we reach the mountain wall again. Turn left once more, following the wall until we come to the gate where we rejoin the main plantation road.

Go through the gate and follow the track over the shoulder of Cronk Fedjag (hill of the plover) to join the Sloc Road, turn right through the gate and follow the surfaced road for a short distance to the corner. Go straight on and follow the unsurfaced track downhill to a crossroads with a cattle grid and gate on the left. We turn right and take the road alongside the Kerrowdhoo Plantation.

Some years ago, I was involved in a project promoted by Geoff Duke, the former World Champion motorcyclist, for a race course in this area, to replace the TT course, which was considered to be under threat from pressure of development, and to comply with stringent rules being introduced controlling the safety of motor racing circuits for World Championship events. It all seems a long time ago now and I am reminded of my mother telling me about watching the TT Races from the field hedges adjoining Bray Hill. My grandchildren will be hearing the same tale from me about Signpost Corner! Anyway, if the project had reached fruition we might have been walking along the start/finish straight of a full-blown Formula One race course instead of a rutted old track.

Keep an eye out for the first gate on the left, leading into the plantation. Here it is — it is rough but fairly easy going and all downhill. After about half a mile, it levels out for a short distance in a clearing among the trees. Look to the right — this is quite definitely a hidden corner. The plantation covers a cirque-like valley formed by tremendous water run-off from the adjoining hills. This valley can not be appreciated from anywhere else and is worth more than a passing glance. In fact, a good lunch stop! The river which runs down the valley now is only a shadow of the one which formed it. Starting from a spring above the road, it quickly grows in strength as it is fed by a number of tributaries until it becomes the Kylley River. It takes its name from one of the ruined farms on the opposite side of the valley. The farm has an obscure name similar to the Kella in Lezayre, which seems to relate to an island formed between two of the tributaries.

Continue down the track which steepens as it emerges at Kerroodhoo (a common Manx place name, meaning Black Quarterland), which is a long-disused farm, now in ruins. At the end of the winter, just before spring gets under way, the old farm garden is covered with snowdrops which give way within a month or so to a carpet of daffodils. I often wonder who planted them — and the fuchsia, which, although unkempt, still line the farmyard, despite recent forestry activities. If you walk out into the cleared area, you will have another unusual view of the valley below Dalby Mountain, which is the source of the Lagg River (river of the hollow), which joins the Kylley River to disgorge to the sea down a spectacular staircase of little waterfalls below Cregganmooar.

Before leaving Kerrowdhoo, look at the ruined building in what was the farmyard and you will see the remains of a mill. On top of the bank behind the buildings are the well preserved remains of the gearing and shaft from the horse mill which was used by the family that worked the farm.

The way out of the plantation is obvious as it follows the wide forest road to the gate where we cross a stepping stile to join the shared access road to the Lagg Road, respecting the privacy of those who live on there. After a short distance, we join the Lagg Road and turn right to follow it past the large farmhouse at Ballacooil and join the main road down to Dalby village to wait for the bus back to Douglas, via Peel. If you have a long wait, it is worth walking down to Niarbyl (or more correctly, "yn arbyl", meaning the tail). The views down the coast across Niarbyl Bay are quite spectacular.

If you are really energetic, you can follow the coastal path to Glen Maye and on to Peel and return to Douglas from there, but it will take another $1^1/_2$ to $1^3/_4$ hours to get to Peel, so study the bus timetable carefully before making the decision.

Turf and surf!

Walk

16

7 hours
15 miles

An inland walk from Douglas to Laxey, which should also provide food for more than just thought, for the gourmets among us.

LET'S start this walk at the Sea Terminal in Douglas, but before moving off, we should give the building more than a passing look. It was built in the early 1960s, and won a premier architectural award. It replaced an old Victorian arcade known affectionately as "the triangle". The old building, built in red brick, had an arcade of shops, surrounded by a glazed canopy supported on wrought iron columns and glazing bars, a waiting hall with an ornate fountain, toilets, barber's shop, all sur-

The old "triangle" shortly before demolition in 1961

mounted by a beautiful clock tower. Short memories let us forget how busy this area was, with its interchange of passengers, buses, taxis and horse trams.

In the decade after the second world war, it was clear that the old building was inadequate and a new terminal was needed. It was slow coming and when it was finally built, the passenger arrivals had declined and car ferries were changing the pattern of travel. The terminal building never achieved its full potential as a passenger handling facility, but it now houses the Tourism Department and the Technical Services function of the Department of Highways, Ports and Properties, and so it has achieved a better balance of use.

Now, let us head out of town, passing the bus station, Lord Street and the Railway Station. If I tried to point out all the places of architectural interest, we would never get out of Douglas, but look at Coronation Terrace, Hanover Street Board School and Lord Street flats. Carry on up Peel Road and out to the Quarterbridge passing the Central Fire Station, with its unique style, before crossing the road at the Quarterbridge to join the old railway line to Peel, now part of the Heritage Trail. The first part of the old track provides an access road to the inside of the TT Course when the public roads are closed for racing. No, the old railway line did not climb up and down like a switchback (*see illustration on page 16*) before going under the road bridge at Braddan. That earthwork was built after the railway closed to provide support for the roadway.

Carry straight on to Union Mills and, as we swing round into the site of the old station, look out for the Gibbons breakdown crane of the original Isle of Man Railway which now forms the central feature at the old station. We cross the River Dhoo on a footbridge, passing an industrial estate where, if you look carefully, you will see traces of the buildings from which the village obtained its name.

As we leave the village, we swing round into the broad valley of the River Dhoo. The central valley is very wet in this locality and iris and willow abound. So do tadpoles in season. We must look out for the point where Cadmans Glen, or Glenlough, joins the railway. The track runs straight to the gatehouse at Closemooar crossing which you will see in the distance. There is an avenue of trees on the left, two metal gates opposite each other and a glen on the right. This is where we are going, through the gate and up the track to the main Douglas to Peel road. Although not a public right of way, this track is much used by local people and provided the gates are closed after you have gone through, you should have no trouble.

At the main road, be careful — the traffic is very fast and we must cross to the other side, turning right and walking along the footway until we come to the right of way sign before the farm, which takes us left over a stile into the field at Ballafreer. I almost forgot to mention as we walked up Glenlough that its proper name is Glion Logh, meaning Lake Glen. You will remember when we talked about the northern loughs that I mentioned that there were also many in the central valley, all formed at the same time but now only surviving in the place names.

We must be careful we don't lose our way through Ballafreer: consult the map, it should also be waymarked, and look out for the white lady in stone on the corner of the hedge where the farm road joins from the right. The path is diverted around the farm buildings and, once in the fields to the

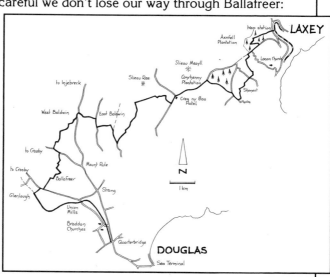

rear of the farm, you should look for the next waymarker and refer to the map. Eventually we emerge on Trollaby Lane, where we turn left and walk uphill to join the Mount Rule Road, going left for a short distance, passing two farm workers' cottages on the right, before turning right over the Rhyne Road. The road quickly degenerates into an unsurfaced track and turns away from Greeba which has been ahead of us.

We walk on the level for a while before starting a descent, where the track becomes considerably rougher. The views ahead, of the flanks of Greeba, Colden and Carraghyn, and over the West Baldwin valley, are best seen from here. At the bottom of the hill, we cross a small stream draining from Ballalough (farm of the lakes)— think about the meaning of the place name in this location. Go up the hill and right at the junction at the top. The road is now surfaced and we follow it to West Baldwin village. Ahead is Carraghyn and visible on the hillside is St Luke's Chapel, or Keeill Aban. Once in the village, we walk left as far as the bridge over the River Glass. Cross the bridge and look for the right of way sign on the right which will take us to the East Baldwin valley. We have just crossed the trackbed of the Injebreck reservoir tramway and one of the quarries used in obtaining material lies behind the old chapel on the corner. The tramway had to cross from West Baldwin to East Baldwin, to the clay pits at Abbeylands, and this is where that part of the trackbed left the West Baldwin valley and followed the river.

We head up above the house, following the right of way on the edge of a shallow escarpment above the river for a short while, then turning left over the fields to East Baldwin, joining the road by means of a very old stone stile. Turning right, we walk back down the road a short distance passing the old school, now a private residence, looking out for the right of way sign on the left at Renscault, which diverts the path around a house before it crosses the Baldwin River and heads up the side of the valley. If the river is in spate, the best way to cross is boots off and round your neck! Look for the old farmhouse at Balliargey (a corruption of Balley liargee, "the farm on the slope"). It seems a little forlorn in the trees but it must have been a grand mansion in its day. Follow the track from the farm to what I know as the Strenaby Road and follow that to the right at the forked junction, continuing down to the Abbeylands Chapel on the Abbeylands Road.

We go left here, out almost to Lanjaghan Farm, turning left at the end of the surfaced road, then along the unsurfaced road uphill to the windswept trees, almost to the mountain wall. Here the track turns right, and skirts the flank of Slieau Ree (the red mountain), sometimes referred to as Keppel Mountain, above Lanjaghan. There are some good views over Douglas from here.

Lanjaghan Lane emerges on the TT Course, just below the world famous Creg ny Baa Hotel (the name means "hill of the cow"). We head up the road to the Creg, which is a public house and a first class restaurant. In fact it is an ideal stop for a pub lunch. Some of the history of the place and its connections with motor cycling can be seen in the photographs exhibited on the walls.

Suitably refreshed, we continue on our way, leaving the TT Course and walking along the Creg ny Baa back road. This section of road too was used for motorcycling between 1954 and 1959, as part of the Clypse Circuit. Would you believe as you walk along a short section of it that it was introduced for sidecar racing.

Continue until we come to the Conrhenny Plantation — it is quite obvious, and a well-defined track leads off the road to the right. Be careful to take the left fork a little way along. We follow the edge of the plantation until we join the surfaced Begoade Road, walking along the top of the hedge to avoid the pond just before the road. Go straight on to the next bend and straight on again down the narrow road ahead, and look out for the right of way on the left, leading to Shonest (or, more correctly, "Hoanes" — the meaning is obscure, but probably Icelandic in origin). Follow the signs and the map carefully, pass the farm buildings, go through the gate opposite the barn and follow the grass track between the hedges, with one signposted diversion through a boggy portion, to Ballaskerroo. The path goes round the back of the barn and we walk over an old horse mill before crossing a stile into the farmyard. After passing through Ballaskerroo, the path joins the Ballagawne Road which we cross, following the right of way signs to Ballacogeen and left to Pooil Villa, being careful not to miss the dogleg at the end, where the right of way emerges onto the Creg ny Baa back road at Social Cottage. Then it is right up the hill, straight on over the top towards Laxey.

But, you have guessed — it would be too easy to go straight on to Laxey. Look for the right of way sign to the left, through Axenfel Plantation and down what must be the steepest footpath on the Island, following a dilapidated stone wall. I well remember the first time I walked this path. I was going up it in a violent thunderstorm, checking the route for the provisional rights of way maps. It is indelibly etched on my memory! If your knees do not feel up to the steep path, you can follow the broad track in a big left-right zigzag, but be careful not to lose your way at the bottom. You should come out at a bridge, crossing the Glen Roy river, and you are now in the Laxey Glen Gardens. Turn right and follow the river to the village and the tram station for a ride back to Douglas, or the bus in winter, as the walk is quite a long one. Consult the timetable — you may have to wait in the Mines Tavern.

Oh, the title of this walk?

Well all the walks in the book relate in some way either to surf or turf, but this is the only one where you can sample real "surf and turf"* dishes at the Creg ny Baa.

You can't keep a good man from his food! Happy walking and enjoy yourselves.

* *That's fish and meat to the non-cogniscenti!*

_____

Useful information

Museums

The Manx Museum, Crellin's Hill, Douglas. Headquarters of the national museum service and the Manx National Trust, with extensive collections ranging from prehistory to the present day. Building also houses the National Art Gallery and the National Reference Library. ☎ 675522

Grove Museum of Rural Life, Ramsey. Fine Victorian residence with period displays. Buses 20A and 20B from Ramsey.

Nautical Museum, Castletown. Main feature is the 18th century armed yacht, Peggy. Steam railway or buses 1, 1A and 8 to Castletown.

Cregneash Village Folk Museum. Housed in traditional restored Manx cottages. Bus 1A

Murrays Motorcycle Museum. A must for TT fans. Bungalow station, Snaefell Railway. ☎ 781719

Crosby Motor Museum. Remarkable collection of vintage vehicles. Bus 5 or 6. ☎ 851236

Laxey Heritage Trust (for information on the Mines Trail). Manx Electric Railway to Laxey. ☎ 862007

Odin's Raven. Replica Viking long boat, Peel harbour. ☎ 843300

Railway museums

Steam railway, Port Erin station. **Electric railway**, Ramsey station. **Trams**, Douglas Corporation terminus, Derby Castle. Department of Transport, ☎ 663366.

Transport

Railways: Strathallan Crescent, Douglas ☎ 663366
Bus station: Lord Street, Douglas ☎ 662525
Tourist information ☎ 686766
Isle of Man Steam Packet Seaways ☎ 661661
Manx Airlines ☎ 824313

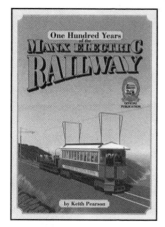